Stefan Buczacki

Best Summer Flowering Shrubs

Special Photography Andrew Lawson

HAMLYN

Publishing Director Laura Bamford
Executive Editor Julian Brown
Assistant Editor Karen O'Grady
Design Manager Bryan Dunn
Designer TT Designs
Production Josephine Allum
Picture Research Jenny Faithfull
Special Photography Andrew Lawson
Research Hilary Engel

First published in Great Britain in 1997
by Hamlyn
an imprint of Reed International Books Limited
Michelin House, 81 Fulham Road, London SW3 6RB
and Auckland, Melbourne, Singapore and Toronto

Printed in Hong Kong

A catalogue record for this book is available from
the British Library

ISBN 0 600 590240

CONTENTS

INTRODUCTION

The irresistible rise and rise of the shrub must, surely, be the characteristic feature of twentieth century gardening. In earlier times, shrubs appeared in gardens very largely as isolated specimens or else in rather formal and dismal groups, generally of evergreen foliage species. They then moved into the herbaceous border and began to burst into flower, at first sitting alongside, and then, in large measure displacing the herbaceous perennials themselves. Now the shrub is the supreme inhabitant of our gardens, and the modern shrub is far from being simply a foliage plant: in many of the gardens that I see today, the majority of the flowers are those borne on shrubs.

The range of shrub species and varieties has never been larger and the colour spectrum never wider. The possible planting combinations and mixtures are now seemingly endless and, because of the vast numbers now available, I have limited my scope in this book to those shrubs that flower in the summer months. I have, however, defined my limits generously to include some shrubs that begin flowering in the spring and the many that don't finish flowering until the autumn.

To justify its inclusion in a garden, a plant should ideally offer something of interest for as long as possible, so only the most stunning summer-flowering shrubs justify their inclusion in a small garden by virtue of their flowers alone. I have indicated in my descriptions, therefore, the appeal that my selected shrubs offer beyond their flowering period: evergreen foliage, autumn leaf colour, attractive fruits or buds, for example.

Summer-flowering shrubs can appeal in a variety of ways, and I have tried to include information on colour, flower size and fragrance in my lists of Recommended Varieties. The flowering shrub can offer any colour that you can imagine; and a few shades that you really can't. In a few genera, and even within some individual species, the colour range is wide; *Potentilla fruticosa*, for instance, can supply you with flowers in white, yellow, pink, orange or red. In most cases, the colour range is much more limited; red and blue or purple are often found together in the same species, as are yellow and orange. Green is pretty rare and generally accompanies white, although pure white forms are to be found in almost every shrub type; the variety 'Alba' must be one of the commonest in all of horticulture.

Flower size can vary greatly, each type and size of flower having its own

Chaenomeles x superba 'Crimson and Gold'

attraction. In my selection, *Hypericum forrestii* probably has some of the largest single flowers, and *Holodiscus discolor* among the smallest. But who is to say which is the prettier or more appealing? And of course, in many shrubs, small flowers are grouped together into flowerheads or inflorescences which can exceed any individual bloom in size. The inflorescences of *Buddleia davidii* or *Hydrangea paniculata* 'Grandiflora', for instance, may exceed 30cm (12in) in length. Fragrance is really in the nose of the beholder and, mostly, I haven't attempted to describe it. If a shrub strikes me as pleasingly and significantly fragrant, I have said so without further elaboration.

There are many plants that span the boundary between shrubs and trees and also between shrubs and herbaceous perennials. It's useful to think of a tree as a woody plant that exceeds about 6m (20ft) in height on a single stem. A few of the plants that I have included may do this in time or if trained, pruned (or not pruned) in particular ways. At the other extreme, some plants that are fairly low growing, have only moderately woody stems and may be cut down to soil level for best effect each season and could, with some justification, be called herbaceous perennials. Shrubs are now indispensable components of the modern garden. They require relatively little care and attention and, in this respect, are ideal for people who have little time or inclination to spend in gardening. But they are indispensable also in the way that they can be used with almost every other garden plant to create an impact.

Opposite: *Choisya ternata*

USING FLOWERING SHRUBS IN THE GARDEN

Let's first consider the blending of different types of flowering shrub in the garden. You should choose types that are compatible in terms of growth rate and ultimate size. Two young shrubs may look very similar in their pots at the garden centre but one may swamp the other in a couple of years in your garden unless you have checked their growth characteristics carefully. For a small garden, you should select types that have as long a flowering period as possible. But in these circumstances, you must be especially careful in your choice of colours when planting. The juxtaposition of two clashing reds or oranges can be extremely distressing

Cestrum parqui

and, in limited space, you may simply be unable to position the plants far enough apart to avoid this.

In a larger garden, length of flowering period is less important and you can select shrubs with shorter but overlapping or consecutive flowering periods. A good way to achieve this is to note when the flowers on each particular shrub in your garden are fading and then select something else that is just opening its buds. And, of course, with greater space and shorter individual flowering periods, colour clashes are more easily avoided.

Flowering shrubs blend particularly well with foliage shrubs (see Book 2, *Best Foliage Shrubs*). Bear in mind that a shrub with large flowers or flower-

heads but small leaves can 'borrow' the leaves of an adjacent shrub to set off the blooms. Evergreen foliage shrubs are particularly valuable in this respect, forming a permanent framework.

In a mixed border, flowering shrubs complement herbaceous perennials perfectly although, here also, the potential for colour clashes and conflicting flowering times should be borne in mind. Give especially careful thought to positioning in respect of size. If you plant your shrubs in the dormant winter season, your herbaceous perennials will be all but invisible. By the summer, they could be 2m (6½ft) tall and your shrubs will have vanished from view.

Bulbs make excellent companions for summer-flowering shrubs, especially if

you choose small spring and autumn flowering species. They can be planted very close to the shrubs to give interest when the shrubs themselves are out of flower. They work perhaps best of all if the bulbs are planted beneath the branches of deciduous species; by the time that the shrubs come into leaf, the crocuses, cyclamen or other small bulbs will be fading.

Summer-flowering shrubs can be used with annuals, too, but be careful. The yearly planting and digging up of annuals inevitably involves soil disturbance, which can result in damage to the roots of the shrubs and possibly stimulate some to begin producing annoying suckers. In my garden, I find that growing annuals in pots and then

positioning these among and close to shrubs is a much more satisfactory option; and, of course, the pots of annuals can then be replaced with others as the plants within them fade.

This brings me, finally, to the growing of shrubs in containers. As I explained in Book 8, *Best Container Plants*, any plant can be grown in a container and flowering shrubs are no exception. You will find further guidance in that book, but choice, individual specimens placed in a prominent position are especially effective. With container plants, especially those in large immovable containers, length of flowering period is important unless the plant also has stunningly attractive foliage to carry on the interest for the rest of the season.

Above: *Kerria japonica* '**Pleniflora**'
Below: *Hydrangea aspera* '**Villosa**'

SOIL AND SITE

A flowering shrub that doesn't flower or that does so feebly and inadequately is a frustration and a waste of money and space. Some shortcomings may be corrected by appropriate feeding (see page 10) or by the control of pests or diseases (page 14), but many a basic error is made in the initial site and planting.

Patently, all shrubs grow in soil but the type of soil that suits one may not suit another. While some shrubs may perform well in one garden or one locality, they may not do so in another for reasons that aren't necessarily obvious. Let's look first at soil.

Soil isn't a homogeneous mass of brown stuff. It is a highly complex medium with many different components. There are four main solid ingredients: on one hand the mineral particles, which are divided, in decreasing size, into sand, silt and clay, and on the other, the organic matter or humus. In addition, there are the more transient, non-solid components such as water and air together with greater or lesser numbers of a myriad different living organisms.

Because of the unique physical properties of the minute particles that make up clay, a soil with a high clay content will be slow to warm up in spring but then retains warmth well and is likely to be generously supplied with nutrients. In dry conditions, it can be hard and impenetrable whereas in wet winter weather, it may become waterlogged. By contrast, a light sandy soil will warm up quickly, cool down quickly and, being free-draining, lose both water and nutrients rapidly.

While some types of shrub will be more tolerant of clayey soils and others more tolerant of sandy ones, almost all shrubs will benefit if extreme soils are improved. Humus (part-decomposed organic matter) will do this for both types of soil because it contains natural glues that bind the soil particles together to form crumbs, and also helps with the retention of moisture because of its sponge-like properties. You should, therefore, always dig in plenty of compost, manure or other organic matter before planting.

The planting position should be prepared by digging a hole of approximately twice the volume of the pot ball of compost if the plant is in a container or twice the root spread of one that is bare-rooted or root-balled. The soil removed should be mixed with a roughly equal volume of compost or similar organic matter and a few handfuls of bonemeal. The phosphate in this aids root development and will help the plant to establish quickly.

If the plant is bare-rooted, the roots should be spread carefully in the planting hole and any that are wayward or crossing, cut off. Gently replace the soil and compost mixture in the hole, moving the plant up and down if necessary to ensure that no air pockets remain

Syringa vulgaris 'Madame Lemoine'

Leycesteria formosa

Romneya coulteri

among the roots. I always prefer to tease away the roots lightly around the edge of the compost ball of a plant from a container as otherwise they tend to grow inwards, towards the generally more moist compost in the centre rather than out into the surrounding soil. Firm the soil carefully with your boot as you fill the hole but don't ram it down too hard. And finally, ensure that you finish by making a small mound with the soil sloping away from the plant's stem. This will prevent water from collecting at the base, freezing and causing damage. Water the plant well after planting.

There is another important aspect of soils that you will need to take account of with many types of shrub: its relative acidity or alkalinity. This is usually expressed as its pH on a scale from 0 to 14. Soils with a pH above 7 are alkaline, those with a pH below 7, acid. Most soils are naturally somewhere between about pH 6 and pH 7.5 (more or less neutral) and most shrubs will thrive in these conditions, but there are numerous exceptions. *Crinodendron* and *Gaultheria* are among the many types of summer-flowering shrub that must have an acidic soil while many others will survive rather inadequately if the soil is too alkaline. By contrast, a few shrubs, such as *Spartium* are very much better in more alkaline conditions.

The pH of a slightly acid soil can be raised fairly simply by adding lime. A strongly acid soil is unlikely to be changed to any significant degree and unfortunately, a procedure that would be very valuable, that of decreasing the pH of a naturally alkaline soil, is also very difficult to do. You will make

Kolkwitzia amabilis

some progress by incorporating sulphur chips which are sold for the purpose but a naturally very alkaline soil is unlikely to be changed to any significant extent.

The site of flowering shrubs is generally more straightforward than that of foliage species. While many plants will grow well in the sun and many will also thrive in shade, very few will flower satisfactorily in shady places. The majority of the plants in this book should, therefore, be sited in full sun; light or dappled shade is as much as they will tolerate. I do recommend light shade, however, for a few species whose flower colour tends to fade in hot sun or whose leaves are so delicate that they scorch. They tend to be species of natural woodland.

CARE OF FLOWERING SHRUBS

No plant will give of its best without at least a little care and attention. Some flowering shrubs are, however, much less demanding than others and will manage with little care, and even tolerate a degree of abuse and serious neglect. Others must be looked after rather more fastidiously.

Allowing for the shrub having been planted in well-prepared soil and in an appropriate site (page 8), what else can be done? Although the soil provides any plant with its basic nutrients, a garden plant, as I have said on many occasions, requires rather more if it is to give full satisfaction. The 'rather more' is provided through the medium of fertilizer but it's worth appreciating that the different ingredients of a fertilizer have different roles.

Of the three major nutrient substances, nitrogen (N) encourages leafy growth, potash (K) encourages fruiting and flowering, and phosphate (P) encourages root development. It's misleading, of course, to try to look at each in isolation. No plant will function properly without vigorous, actively growing foliage, so nitrogen really is the key element and it must be present in any fertilizer but a relatively high dose of potash will be particularly helpful, too, for flowering. Fortunately, these requirements are readily satisfied by the proprietary blends sold as rose fertilizer. Roses are generally fed twice a year; once after the spring pruning and once in early summer after the first flush of flowers has faded. Feed all of your flowering shrubs at the same times and in the same way and they will be well satisfied.

Those shrubs that require acidic soils, or that tend to grow better in

Cassia (Senna) corymbosa

Phygelius capensis

them, will benefit from an additional fertilizer application in the early spring using a product containing sequestered iron. This is iron in an organic form that plants can absorb easily, even in alkaline conditions. Without iron, plants are unable to manufacture the green colouring material chlorophyll and so are unable to phoyosynthesize and grow effectively.

There are a few other important rules of shrub care worth considering. Water is as important for shrubs as it is for other plants but, once established, most have relatively deep root systems and should survive through most summers provided they have been well mulched with organic matter in the early part of the season, when the soil is still moist. When young, of course, a shrub needs as much attention to watering as any other young plant.

It's often thought that, because they are relatively big and relatively robust, shrubs are well able to compete effectively with weeds. Some shrubs, indeed, are sold on the strength of a weed-suppressing, ground-covering capability. Sadly, this is one of gardening's more enduring myths. There are a very few shrubs that can smother the ground and most weeds in the process; *Hypericum calycinum* (page 56) is the best known. Most are much less efficient and most, when young, can't compete effectively with anything. So weed control in the shrubbery is important and is most readily achieved with blanket mulching; that is, mulching over the entire border. Ideally this should consist of a 10cm (4in) deep layer of organic matter but, if such quantities are unavailable, a thick mulch around the base of the plant and a thinner layer spread over a synthetic, porous mulching sheet will suffice.

Because most shrubs, by definition, tend not to be single-stemmed, they rarely need support although any trained as standards will require a stake, at least when young. The stem should be secured to the stake with a small, belt-style tree tie.

Abutilon x *suntense* **should have the oldest third of the shoots cut out every spring**

PRUNING AND PROPAGATION

Pruning is important with some types of flowering shrub; less so with others. But the thought that you might have to do some shouldn't put you off growing any shrub, for it is a simple, common-sense operation to be performed once a season.

Pruning involves cutting off parts of plants. Clearly, this reduces their size but more importantly, it stimulates other parts to grow. The buds at the end or apex of a stem exert a chemical growth-suppressing influence on other buds further down. This is called apical dominance. Cut off the end of a stem, therefore, and those other buds will burst into life. If they are leaf buds, you will have foliage further down the stem; if they are flower buds, more bloom. And sometimes, some pruning away of the apex is usefully combined with bending the stem down to the horizon-tal, this also helping to diminish apical dominance and stimulate more uniform leaf or flower production.

Cutting away a large proportion of a plant is called hard pruning; cutting away a little is called light pruning. In general, you should hard prune those plants that are the less vigorous grow-ers. This is simply because, in stimulat-ing bud development as I've described, pruning generates more growth.

Regardless of the amount of stem to be removed, pruning cuts should always be made just above a bud, leaf, flower, branch fork or other actively growing structure, never in the middle of a stem or branch. This ensures that the cut surface heals quickly and doesn't merely wither and allow decay organisms to enter. On other than very slender stems, the cut should be sloped away from the bud or other organ, but not so close as to damage it; about 5mm (¼in) above is generally safe. Even on large woody stems, never apply a wound sealing compound. These were once considered a benefit but are now thought at best useless and at worst positively harmful.

The timing of pruning flowering shrubs is rather critical. If you prune at the wrong time, you won't do long-term damage but you will cut away a good many of the flower buds and the operation will become self-defeating. I give basic pruning advice under the individual descriptions but stick to the following guidelines and you won't go far wrong. Summer-flowering shrubs bear their flowers in one of two ways: those that flower before midsummer generally do so on shoots that grew during the previous season; those that flower after midsummer usually do so on shoots produced during the current year. You should always, therefore, prune *after* flowering. Another useful general rule is that the later in the year the shrub flowers, the harder it should be pruned. Thus early summer-flower-ing shrubs need light pruning as their flowers fade, while late summer-flow-ering shrubs need more severe pruning and, although this may be done imme-diately after flowering, it is very often better left until early in the following spring because the old shoots will give valuable protection in the winter.

Good pruning is achieved with good tools and no gardener can manage without a pair of secateurs or pruners. Select between the single-bladed anvil pattern which is best for hard woody stems but tend to crush softer ones, and the two-bladed scissor or by-pass type which is less robust but more gen-

Cestrum parqui

tle in action. Ideally, you should have both. If you have large shrubs with stout woody stems, you will also require a pair of loppers which, in essence, are long-handled secateurs for thicker branches and are also available in both anvil or by-pass style. You may even occasionally need to resort to something stronger still and a curved pruning saw may be necessary on really big and tough shrubs that verge on tree size. As with all garden tools, I can do no more than repeat the advice that I have given on many other occasions: buy the best that you can afford. The difference between good and poor quality cutting tools is more marked than with most other types of gardening equipment.

Hydrangea macrophylla **'Mariesii Perfecta'**

Propagation

While the propagation of flowering shrubs is very rarely essential, it is always rewarding and so I have included brief notes on the best methods under the individual descriptions. The basic methods are outlined below.

Cuttings

There are three main types of cuttings: softwood, which are taken in early summer; semi-ripe, taken as the shoots mature in late summer; and hardwood, taken in late autumn. Apart from hardwood cuttings, all types should be rooted (or 'struck') in a covered chamber, either a small heated propagator or a covered cold frame. It is very important to maintain a moist atmosphere around the cuttings for they will otherwise lose water through their leaves at a time when, lacking roots,

they are unable to replace it from below. The cold frame can also be used for hardwood cuttings although I prefer to root these in a sheltered spot in the open garden, inserting the shoots in a narrow 'V' shaped trench in the bottom of which I have layered some sand. Cuttings of all types should be removed from the parent plant with a clean cut made just below a bud.

Layering

Propagating evergreen shrubs can present problems for, even if cuttings are taken during their dormant season, the presence of leaves means that water will still be lost at a time when the plant has no means of replacing it, because of the lack of roots. The difficulty can often be overcome by layering: anchoring a stem into the soil while it is still attached to the parent plant. The disadvantage is that some patience

is needed as layerings rarely root satisfactorily in less than 18 months.

Seed

Some types of flowering shrub can be raised from seed although it has to be said that many of the best are selected varieties that may not produce any seed, or that produce seed which subsequently gives rise to variable offspring. Almost invariably, seed of woody plants is best stratified before it will germinate. This simply means sowing it in a container of very sandy, free-draining compost and leaving it in a cold frame or completely outdoors over winter. Once it has been subjected to frost in this way, the inbuilt dormancy mechanism will be overcome and germination will proceed when the seeds are brought into warmth in the spring, ideally in a propagator.

PESTS AND DISEASES

Every kind of garden plant is prone to pests and diseases; flowering shrubs are no exception but, overall, they are not especially prone to attack and certainly fare much better than plants with masses of soft and fleshy tissues such as bulbs, fruit, vegetables and annuals. Treatment is rather seldom called for and, in my own garden, I very rarely use chemical controls on flowering shrubs but it is useful to understand the relative importance of the different types of problem and to know what options are available if serious damage does occur. I have discussed the subject in much greater detail in Book 9 of this series, *Best Garden Doctor* and what follows is only a brief summary.

Problem	Detail	Probable cause
Symptoms on flowers		
a. Drooping	General End of flowering period	Short of water
b. Tattered	Masses of tiny holes Large pieces torn away	Caterpillars Birds
c. Removed entirely	Usually discarded nearby	Birds
d. Discoloured	Powdery white covering	Mildew
e. Mouldy	Fluffy, grey	Grey mould (*Botrytis*)
Symptoms on leaves		
a. Wilting	General	Short of water Wilt disease Root pest or disease
b. Holed	Generally ragged Elongate holes Fairly large holes over entire leaf or confined to edges	Small pests (millepedes, woodlice), capsid bugs Slugs or snails usually with slime present Caterpillars, beetles, birds
c. Discoloured	Black Predominantly red More or less bleached Short of water Irregular yellowish patterns Irregular tunnels Surface flecking Brown (scorched) in spring	Sooty mould Short of water Fertilizer deficiency Too much water Virus (but check that not a variegated variety) Leaf miners Leafhoppers Frost
d. Spotted	Brown-black, irregular, no mould Small, dusty, brown, black or brightly coloured	Leaf spot Rust
e. Mouldy	Black Grey, fluffy White, (or rarely brown),	Sooty mould Grey mould Mildew velvety
f. Infested with tiny insects	White, moth-like, Green, grey, black or other colour Flat, encrusted, like limpets Large, six legs, worm-like	Whiteflies Aphids Scale insects Caterpillars
g. Cobwebs present	Leaves also discoloured	Red spider mites

Symptoms on stems or branches

a. Eaten through	On young plants	Slugs or snails
	On older plants	Mice, voles, rabbits
b. Infested with insects	Green, grey, black or other colour	Aphids
	Flat, encrusted, like limpets	Scale insects
	Large, six legs, worm-like	Caterpillars
c. Rotten	At base, young plants	Stem and foot rot
	On mature shrubs	Decay fungus
d. Blister on stems	More or less spherical	Gall
	Target-like	Canker
e. Dying back	General	Short of water
		Root pest or disease
		Canker or coral spot

Treatments for common pest and disease problems on flowering shrubs

Problem	Treatment
Aphids	Use any proprietary contact insecticide; pick off affected shoots by hand or wash off insects with hose
Beetles	Normally, treatment is not necessary or justified but in cases of extensive attack use any proprietary contact insecticide
Birds	Erect netting or other protection; in really severe cases, erect bird scarers but remember that all birds enjoy legal protection and may not be harmed
Canker	Cut out and destroy affected branches; no chemical treatment is possible
Capsid bugs	Too unpredictable and erratic in occurrence to make any treatment feasible
Caterpillars	Pick off by hand if the caterpillars can be found and are present in small numbers. If masses of insects occur, pick off and destroy entire affected leaves or use any proprietary contact insecticide
Coral spot	Cut away and destroy affected branches or twigs, cutting well into the healthy wood. On very valuable flowering shrubs, then spray the surrounding branches with a systemic fungicide
Fertilizer deficiency	Give general balanced liquid fertilizer
Fungal decay	Cut out and destroy affected parts; no other treatment is feasible
Gall	Normally no treatment is justified but cut out if severely disfiguring
Grey mould	Destroy affected parts; spray with systemic fungicide
Leaf hopper	Too erratic and unpredictable to make any treatment practicable
Leaf miner	Remove and destroy affected leaves on herbaceous plants
Leaf spot	In most instances no treatment is necessary for leaf spot diseases are rarely severe. Where attacks appear to be related to general poor growth, however, spray with systemic fungicide
Mice	Set traps or use proprietary poison baits
Mildew	Ensure that plants are not allowed to become too dry and apply systemic fungicide or sulphur

Problem	Treatment
Millepedes	Dust in affected area with derris
Rabbits	The only sure protection is by using a wire netting fence with the lower edge turned outwards at 90° over the soil surface
Red spider mite	No treatment is really feasible although keeping plants well watered and mulched will help limit the impact of attacks
Root pest	Normally, no treatment is feasible but with severe and persistent attacks, dust around affected plants with derris or other soil insecticide
Root disease	Destroy severely affected plants
Rust	Spray with penconazole fungicide
Scale insects	Spray or drench with systemic insecticide
Slugs	Use proprietary slug pellets or liquid controls or home-made remedies such as traps baited with beer. Surround the base of plants with fine powders such as ash or soot or a low barrier of fine spiny twigs such as gorse
Snails	If serious, use methods recommended for slugs but generally they are less serious and fewer in number and can be combated by collecting them by hand and by locating and eradicating them from their hiding places
Sooty mould	Wash off mould with water or destroy badly affected leaves and then identify and treat the insect pest responsible for the honeydew on which the mould grows
Stem and foot rot	Little can be done but as it is often associated with waterlogging, improve drainage of the affected area
Virus	Effects are usually mild, so no treatment is necessary
Voles	Set mouse traps or use proprietary poison baits
Whiteflies	No treatment is feasible on outdoor plants
Wilt disease	No treatment is very effective but drench surrounding soil with systemic fungicide
Woodlice	Dust around plants with proprietary soil insecticide and locate and eradicate them from their hiding places

Abelia

❝ *Abelias are less well-known relatives of honeysuckles, although you wouldn't guess the connection from their flowers, which are much smaller and borne in very attractive clusters. Some are decidedly tender but* Abelia x grandiflora, *a hybrid between two Chinese species has the merit, shared by other plants that flower on the current season's growth that, even if frost causes serious die-back, the new season's blooms aren't lost.* ❞

FLOWERS White, pink or red funnel-shaped flowers borne profusely on current season's wood, sometimes fragrant.
PERIOD OF FLOWERING Early summer to early autumn.
NON-FLOWERING APPEAL Attractive foliage may be tinged with red, or variegated, and may be retained in mild winters.
SITE AND SOIL Prefers full sun but tolerates light shade. Any soil, though less vigorous if very dry or very alkaline.
HARDINESS Hardy, tolerating -15 to -20°C (5 to -4°F).
SIZE 1.2 x 1m (4 x 3ft) after five years; 1.8 x 2m (6 x 6½ft) after 10 years.

■ **PRUNING** On established plants, cut back the oldest one-third of the shoots to soil level each year in spring. Cut back any frost-damaged shoots.
■ **PROPAGATION** Semi-ripe cuttings in late summer.
■ **PROBLEMS** None.

Recommended varieties

A. x *grandiflora* has fragrant white flowers tinged with pink, and very glossy, dark green leaves; its variety 'Francis Mason' has white to pale pink flowers, golden-variegated leaves, is lower growing and slightly more tender. A. *floribunda* has cherry-red flowers in early summer and, being slightly more tender, is best fan-trained against a sunny, sheltered wall.

Abelia x grandiflora

Abutilon

❝ *Ever since I first saw* Abutilon megapotamicum, *growing in a sheltered nook in an otherwise rather cold garden, I have had a very soft spot for abutilons. But to be fair, that rather straggly if striking Brazilian species isn't really typical of the genus; the big bold species like* A. vitifolium *are more representative.* ❞

FLOWERS Conspicuous, often brightly coloured, long-lasting flowers in bell, saucer or lantern shapes.
PERIOD OF FLOWERING Late spring to mid-autumn.
NON-FLOWERING APPEAL Most forms have lush foliage, some evergreen, some attractively variegated.
SITE AND SOIL Needs a sunny, sheltered site, preferably a warm wall or conservatory, or a container that can be brought indoors in winter. Any soil, but ideally rich and well drained.
HARDINESS Many varieties are tender or barely hardy, but those I recommend are at least fairly or moderately hardy, tolerating -10 to -15°C (14 to -4°F) although all will be better with some shelter. May die back in winter, but if dead growth is cut away, they will regenerate from ground level in late spring.
SIZE The smaller forms like A. *megapotamicum* will reach about 1.5 x 1.5m (5 x 5ft) after five years, 2 x 2m (6½ x 6½ft) after 10 years; others, including A. *vitifolium* may grow to twice this size.

Recommended varieties

A. megapotamicum is a slender, tall-growing species bearing bell-shaped flowers with yellow petals, red calyx and purple anthers from late summer to early autumn, its leaves are olive-green with purplish shading and veins; the variegated form is less appealing. *A. vitifolium* is a fast-growing, upright species with saucer-shaped flowers in shades of violet, purple and blue, from late spring to midsummer, and has downy, grey-green vine-shaped leaves. It appears in several varieties including 'Album', which has white flowers tinged with pink; 'Tennant's White', with abundant large pure white flowers; and 'Veronica Tennant', with masses of large lavender flowers. *A. x suntense* is a fast-growing hybrid that bears saucer-shaped flowers in colours ranging from white to deep purple between late spring and midsummer; the very good variety 'Jermyns' has lavender or mauve flowers.

■ **PRUNING** Remove oldest one-third of flowering shoots from established plants in early to mid-spring. Cut back any frost-damaged shoots at the same time.

■ **PROPAGATION** Softwood cuttings in early summer.

■ **PROBLEMS** Frost damage; red spider mites and whiteflies may be serious in warm summers.

Aronia Chokeberry

❝ *I've always assumed that the common name comes from the ability of the very bitter fruit to cause choking in anyone who eats it. But this unpalatability shouldn't dissuade you from growing this shrub if you can offer it the correct conditions. The flowers immediately betray its relationship to the rose family (they remind me of hawthorn) and so it comes as something of a surprise to discover that 'the correct conditions' include acidic soil.* ❞

FLOWERS Small star-shaped white flowers with pronounced red stamens.

PERIOD OF FLOWERING Late spring to late autumn.

NON-FLOWERING APPEAL Brilliant red fruits and autumn foliage.

SITE AND SOIL Needs sun or light shade, and an acid, well-drained soil.

HARDINESS Hardy, tolerating -20°C (-4°F).

SIZE About 1 x 1m (3 x 3ft) after three years, 2-3 x 2m (6½-10 x 6½ft) after 10 years.

■ **PRUNING** None essential, but to achieve best autumn colour, up to one-third of the mature stems may be cut back to soil level in winter.

■ **PROPAGATION** Softwood or semi-ripe cuttings in autumn; also fairly readily from seed.

■ **PROBLEMS** None.

Recommended varieties

Aronia arbutifolia (Red Chokeberry) bears clusters of small white flowers with red anthers, and has dark green foliage that turns red in autumn.

Abutilon x suntense

Aronia arbutifolia

Bauhinia

❝ *Bauhinias are more or less evergreen, but tropical or sub-tropical, only just hardy and not easily obtained, so they might, therefore, be thought not worthy of inclusion in a book of garden shrubs. But so stunning are the flowers of these glorious members of the pea family that anyone who gardens in a mild garden or has a fairly large conservatory should come to know them better. You could even grow one in a large container in the warmest part of your garden and take it under protection in the autumn.* ❞

FLOWERS Orchid like, with protruding 'claws' in large clusters at the ends of lateral shoots.
PERIOD OF FLOWERING Early to late summer.
NON-FLOWERING APPEAL Glossy evergreen foliage.
SITE AND SOIL Needs full sun and fertile, well-drained soil.
HARDINESS Barely hardy, tolerating 0 to -5°C (32-23°F)
SIZE Will slowly attain 3 x 1.5m (10 x 5ft) in warm conditions

■ **PRUNING** Thin out congested growth after flowering and in spring cut out any shoots damaged by cold winds or frost.
■ **PROPAGATION** Semi-ripe cuttings in late summer, or by layering where they can be grown permanently outdoors. Will also grow readily from seed if any can be obtained.
■ **PROBLEMS** None.

Recommended varieties
B. yunnanensis from south-east Asia, has pink to lilac flowers and is generally reckoned the hardiest and most reliable in a temperate climate.

Berberis Barberry

❝ *Berberis, in both its deciduous and evergreen species, has few peers for reliability and quantity of spring flowers. But as a summer flowering shrub it is less commonly considered. A number flower well into the summer in any season with a late spring but I have selected two that do so reliably every year.* ❞

Berberis julianae

■ **PRUNING** For evergreen forms, none essential although misplaced shoots should be cut out in spring. Deciduous forms should have one-third of the oldest stems removed annually in late autumn or winter. Shoots damaged by frost should be cut out in spring.
■ **PROPAGATION** Propagate species by seed in autumn, deciduous hybrids and varieties by softwood or semi-ripe

cuttings in summer, evergreen hybrids and varieties by semi-ripe cuttings in late summer.
■ **PROBLEMS** Normally none although rust can occur occasionally.

FLOWERS Small cup-shaped yellow or orange flowers in large clusters in early summer.
PERIOD OF FLOWERING Spring to autumn.
NON-FLOWERING APPEAL Conspicuous autumn berries, usually red or black, brilliant autumn foliage in deciduous varieties and useful winter colour in evergreen forms. Spiny stems form excellent impenetrable hedges.
SITE AND SOIL Tolerates pollution and also shade, although deciduous forms perform better in sun. Will thrive in most well-drained soils.
HARDINESS Very hardy, tolerating at least -20°C (-4°F).
SIZE Varies with variety, but most will reach about 1.5-2 x 1.5-2m (5-6½ x 5 x 6½ ft) after five years and 2-4m x 2-3m (6½-13 x 6½-10ft) after 10 years.

Recommended varieties
B. aggregata is a deciduous species bearing small double yellow flowers followed by clusters of deep orange-red fruits on two-year-old wood.
B. julianae is a tall species with long spines in groups of three and lemon-yellow flowers; although evergreen, its older leaves may turn brilliant colours and fall in autumn.

Brachyglottis (Senecio)

❝ *It doesn't matter how often they are changed by botanists, some plants will always retain their old names in gardeners' minds. The easy, rather loose-growing but friendly plant that we all grew up to call* Senecio greyi *is one. No matter that it is now* Brachyglottis *'Sunshine', its bright daisy flowers and greyish foliage were all part of our childhood summers and remain in our affections as well as our gardens.* ❞

Recommended varieties
B. 'Moira Read' has creamy-yellow blotches on its leaves; B. 'Sunshine' has silver-grey leaves that mature to dark green. B. monroi has small wavy-edged dark green leaves with white undersides.

FLOWERS Long-lasting white or bright yellow daisy-shaped flowers.
PERIOD OF FLOWERING Flowers in early summer, foliage all year round.
NON-FLOWERING APPEAL Ornate, often woolly, silver-grey, dark green or variegated evergreen foliage.
SITE AND SOIL Prefers full sun or light shade, does particularly well in coastal areas and tolerates most soils as long as they are well drained.
HARDINESS Fairly to moderately hardy, tolerating -10 to -15°C (14 to -4°F).
SIZE The shrubby species reach their maximum size of about 1 x 1.5m (3 x 5ft) after four years.

■ **PRUNING** Trim lightly with shears each spring. Old woody or straggly plants can be rejuvenated if cut back hard in early spring. Frost damaged shoots should also be cut back.
■ **PROPAGATION** Semi-ripe cuttings in summer.
■ **PROBLEMS** Aphids and fungal leaf spots can disfigure the foliage but barely justify control measures.

Brachyglottis 'Sunshine'

BRUNFELSIA

Brunfelsia

❝ *A distinguished name for a distinguished, if little known plant. Otto Brunfels, the sixteenth century botanist was the inspiration; a sub-tropical South American shrub of the potato family is the plant. It is one to move into the garden in summer and under cover in the winter but I include it in order to bring it to the attention of a wider gardening audience.* ❞

FLOWERS Exquisite, fragrant flowers in shades of purple.
PERIOD OF FLOWERING Evergreen foliage and, if kept at a temperature of 13-16°C (55-61°F), the flowers will continue throughout most of the year.
NON-FLOWERING APPEAL Attractive, glossy foliage.
SITE AND SOIL Needs semi-shade and humus-rich, well-drained soil.
HARDINESS Barely hardy, tolerating 0 to -5°C (32-23°F).
SIZE Rarely attains more than 1.5-2 x 1m (5-6½ x 3ft) in Europe.

■ **PRUNING** None essential.
■ **PROPAGATION** Semi-ripe cuttings in summer.
■ **PROBLEMS** Aphids, mealy bugs, whiteflies and other sap-sucking pests.

Recommended varieties
B. pauciflora, sometimes called 'Yesterday-today-and-tomorrow', bears fragrant blue-purple flowers that later fade almost to white, and has lance-shaped, glossy leaves; 'Floribunda' is a smaller, spreading variety with many rich purple-and-white flowers.

Buddleia davidii **'Royal Red'**

Buddleia

❝ *No introduction needed for one of the best-loved of all flowering shrubs; that is, no introduction needed for* Buddleia davidii. *But this familiar Chinese species isn't the beginning and end of the genus and, among many others, anyone with a quite large garden should grow the South American* B. globosa, *the orange-ball tree, a species that was the* buddleia *for European gardens until its oriental relative stole its thunder at the end of the nineteenth century.* ❞

FLOWERS Profuse clusters of small, often fragrant flowers, with many species particularly attractive to butterflies.
PERIOD OF FLOWERING Early to late summer, depending on species.
NON-FLOWERING APPEAL Attractive, dark green or silver-grey foliage; some species are evergreen.
SITE AND SOIL Requires full sun and fertile, well-drained soil although *B. davidii* will thrive in poorer soils.
HARDINESS The species recommended are hardy to very hardy, tolerating at least -5°C (-4°F).
SIZE *B. alternifolia* may reach 4 x 4m (13 x 13ft) unless trained as a weeping standard to about 2.5 x 2.5m (8 x 8ft); the species that are pruned annually, such as *B. davidii*, will reach about 4 x 4m (13 x 13ft) by the end of the season; other species may reach 2 x 2m (6½ x 6½ft) after five years, 4 x 4m (13 x 13ft) after 10 years.

■ **PRUNING** Varies importantly with species. *B. alternifolia* should have all flowering shoots cut back to the base after the flowers have faded; it may have up to one-third of the oldest shoots removed at the same time or instead it may be trained as a weeping standard. *B. davidii*, *B. fallowiana*, *B.* 'Lochinch' and *B.* x *weyeriana* should be cut back hard to about 15cm (6in) above ground level in early spring. Other species may be cut back lightly after flowering.

■ **PROPAGATION** Semi-ripe cuttings in late summer, or hardwood cuttings in winter.

■ **PROBLEMS** Normally none. Capsid bugs may attack leaves but don't merit control measures.

Recommended varieties (all deciduous)

B. alternifolia has gracefully arching branches, covered in early summer with honey-scented lilac-coloured flowers; *B. davidii* varieties bear long racemes of fragrant flowers in mid- to late summer which are particularly attractive to butterflies; 'Black Knight' has deep violet flowers; 'Dartmoor' has magenta flowers; 'Empire Blue' has violet-blue flowers with orange eyes; 'Namho Blue' has pale blue flowers; 'Royal Red' has huge panicles of red-purple flowers; 'White Profusion' has large panicles of white flowers with yellow eyes. *B. fallowiana alba* has cream-white flowers with orange eyes. *B. globosa* (Orange ball tree) has bright orange-yellow balls of flowers in early summer. *B. lindleyana* has long, curved racemes of violet-purple flowers from mid- to late summer. *B.* 'Lochinch' has particularly fragrant violet-blue flowers with orange eyes, and grey young foliage; *B.* x *weyeriana* bears long panicles of orange-yellow ball-shaped flowerheads from mid- to late summer; 'Sungold' has deep orange flowers.

Callistemon Bottlebrush

❝ *Understandably, rather few Australian shrubs are reliably hardy in Britain.* Callistemon, *the bottlebrush will survive only in milder areas. Part of the reason is that the only trustworthy species,* C. citrinus *originates, not from the burning heart of Australia but from cooler, coastal areas.* ❞

FLOWERS Striking red or yellow bottle, brush-shaped flowers.

PERIOD OF FLOWERING Mid- to late summer.

NON-FLOWERING APPEAL Evergreen leaves are aromatic, with a lemon fragrance, and may have red-orange colouring. May produce curious knobbly seedheads.

SITE AND SOIL Full sun, preferably sheltered by a sunny, sheltered wall, or in a large conservatory. Needs a fertile, acid, well-drained soil.

HARDINESS Barely hardy to fairly hardy, tolerating only -5 to -10°C (23 to 14°F).

SIZE About 2 x 1.5m (6½ x 5ft) after five years and twice this after 10 years.

■ **PRUNING** None essential except to remove frost-damaged shoots in spring.

■ **PROPAGATION** Semi-ripe cuttings in late summer.

■ **PROBLEMS** Old plants tend to grow straggly.

Recommended varieties

C. citrinus has bright red flowers; those of the variant 'Splendens' are even more intensely red.

Callistemon citrinus

CALLUNA

Calluna vulgaris Heather, Ling

❝ *Although associated most closely with Scotland, the one-species genus* Calluna *has a natural range far beyond the Highlands, occurring from western North America to Siberia. As individual plants, they are much less spectacular than their close relatives in* Erica, *mainly because the petals are pretty well concealed by the sepals, and* Calluna *is more restricted than* Erica *in its garden usefulness for it has an unvarying need for acidic conditions. But given these, and given room to grow heathers en masse, you have a fine range of varieties from which to select.* ❞

FLOWERS Profuse although tiny flowers in a restricted range of colours.

PERIOD OF FLOWERING Most varieties flower in midsummer, but the dead flowerheads remain attractive through the winter, especially when touched by frost or rime.

NON-FLOWERING APPEAL Evergreen foliage ranging from yellow, gold and purple to dark and light green. Useful ground cover although tending to become straggly and woody with age.

SITE AND SOIL Tolerates partial shade but always thrives best in full sun. Must have acid, moist but free-draining, humus-rich soil.

HARDINESS Very hardy, tolerating below -20°C (-4°F).

SIZE Most species reach their maximum size of about 30 x 30cm (12 x 12in) after eight or nine years although there are few larger and a few smaller forms.

Calluna vulgaris 'Peter Sparkes'

■ **PRUNING** Trim off dead flower-heads in spring using shears.

■ **PROPAGATION** Semi-ripe cuttings in late summer, or layers.

■ **PROBLEMS** The centres of old plants may become brown and woody. To rejuvenate, cut hard back in spring and cover with a mound of soil to stimulate new growth. Plants may be damaged by frost, or drought.

Recommended varieties
C. v. 'Allegro', purple-red flowers; 'Beoley Gold' has white flowers and golden foliage; 'County Wicklow', has double, pale pink flowers; 'Firefly', deep lilac flowers and red-brown foliage that turns orange-red in winter; 'H.E. Beale', one of the finest double-flowered heathers, with tall-stemmed pale pink flowers; 'Kinlochruel', abundant, large, double white flowers; 'Robert Chapman', pale purple flowers and golden foliage that in winter turns to orange and then red, a superb large variety; 'Silver Queen', pale mauve flowers and silvery-grey foliage; 'Wickwar Flame', mauve-pink flowers and bright orange and yellow foliage that turns to copper and gold in winter.

Calycanthus Allspice

❝ *A plant called Allspice sounds as if it must have some culinary or herbal virtue and so it has; some species have been used both in China and by native peoples in North America. It isn't grown in gardens for this purpose today and, indeed, the seeds are distinctly poisonous. To be honest, it isn't grown in gardens very much at all, which is a great pity for its flowers, if not vividly beautiful, are certainly striking and the strong camphor fragrance of the foliage adds greatly to the appeal, especially in hot weather.* ❞

FLOWERS Unusual, rather loosely star-shaped, brownish-red flowers borne on the current year's shoots.
PERIOD OF FLOWERING Throughout summer.
NON-FLOWERING APPEAL The aromatic leaves have good yellow autumn colour in most years.
SITE AND SOIL Prefers light shade but will tolerate full sun. Thrives best on deep, rich soil; intolerant of alkalinity or dryness.
HARDINESS Very hardy, tolerating at least -20°C (-4°F).
SIZE About 1 x 1m (3 x 3ft) after five years, 3 x 3m (10 x 10ft) after 10 years.

■ **PRUNING** None essential.
■ **PROPAGATION** Softwood cuttings in summer.
■ **PROBLEMS** May suffer from die-back in extreme cold.

Recommended varieties
Calycanthus floridus (Carolina all-spice) is the most popular and much the hardiest form, with fragrant brownish-red flowers.

Calycanthus floridus

Caragana Siberian pea tree

❝ *I've had a mission for some years to spread word of this plant. The reason is that I am so often asked for flowering shrubs tolerant of truly harsh conditions; and this is one. Although it is not true of all Siberian plants, this one certainly does tolerate the worst that any temperate climate can offer; and it's tolerant of a wide range of soil types. The flowers aren't spectacular although* en masse, *very pretty. But the overall form of the best varieties is extremely attractive.* ❞

Caragana arborescens 'Lorbergii'

FLOWERS Small yellow and pea-like.
PERIOD OF FLOWERING Early summer.
NON-FLOWERING APPEAL Delicate pinnate foliage and graceful, in some cases weeping, habit.
SITE AND SOIL Needs full sun and fertile but not over-rich soil, tolerates well-drained, even dry, conditions.
HARDINESS Very hardy, tolerating below -20°C (-4°F).
SIZE Varies with variety: *Caragana arborescens* 'Lorbergii' may reach 3 x 2.5m (10 x 8ft), while 'Walker', unless top-grafted, will reach only 30cm x 2-3m (12in x 6½-10ft).

■ **PRUNING** None essential.
■ **PROPAGATION** Propagate the species by softwood cuttings in summer, or by seed in autumn; cultivars by softwood or semi-ripe cuttings or budding in summer or by grafting in winter.
■ **PROBLEMS** None.

Recommended varieties
C. arborescens 'Lorbergii' bears clusters of small yellow flowers and very narrow leaflets, and is often grown as a tree by top-grafting; 'Pendula' is an attractive medium-sized weeping form; 'Walker' is a prostrate shrub that is usually top-grafted to make a small weeping standard with pendent branches.

CARPENTERIA

Carpenteria californica Tree anemone

❝ *I think that I've made more friends through recommending this shrub than any other single plant. People who know it would never garden without it; people who don't, wonder how they have managed. To be fair, coming from a very small area of central California, it isn't particularly hardy although I know of many gardens in mild areas where it has thrived for years. I think, nonetheless, that it is always best, aesthetically as well as practically, as a wall plant.* ❞

FLOWERS Fragrant white saucer-shaped flowers with yellow centres borne on mature wood.
PERIOD OF FLOWERING Early to midsummer.
NON-FLOWERING APPEAL Glossy evergreen foliage.
SITE AND SOIL Preferably full sun, ideally against a sunny, sheltered wall. Needs a fairly moist but free-draining soil; tolerates acid and alkaline conditions.
HARDINESS Fairly to moderately hardy, tolerating around -10°C (14°F). May be some shoot die-back in cold winters.
SIZE 1 x 1m (3 x 3ft) after five years, 1.5 x 1.5m (5 x 5ft) after 10 years.

Recommended varieties
Normal species only is generally available although selected forms with larger flowers are sometimes offered. I have found them less hardy.

■ **PRUNING** Remove one-third of oldest shoots each spring to promote new growth. May be cut back hard to rejuvenate, but this will often mean that the plant can then take two years or more to flower again.
■ **PROPAGATION** Semi-ripe cuttings in summer or seed in autumn.
■ **PROBLEMS** May appear weak when young, but develops quickly after being planted. Be patient, the wait is well worth while.

Carpenteria californica

Caryopteris

❝ *Blue-flowered shrubs are always at a premium because, numerically, there are less of them than there are of any other colour. Two stand out: the North American* Ceanothus *is the better known, but the oriental* Caryopteris *is the other. There are deciduous and evergreen forms of* Ceanothus, *but all* Caryopteris *are deciduous. Against this should be set the fact that the latter are, most valuably, highly tolerant of alkaline conditions which* Ceanothus *are not.* ❞

FLOWERS Clusters of small tubular blue flowers on the current season's shoots.
PERIOD OF FLOWERING Late summer to early autumn.
NON-FLOWERING APPEAL Aromatic grey-green deciduous foliage.
SITE AND SOIL Prefers full sun; in cold areas needs shelter. Any light, well-drained and preferably alkaline soil.
HARDINESS Hardy, tolerating -15°C (5°F).
SIZE Most forms reach about 1.5 x 1m (5 x 3ft).

■ **PRUNING** Cut all shoots back to about 20cm (8in) above soil level or from a larger woody framework in mid- to late spring.
■ **PROPAGATION** Semi-ripe cuttings in early to midsummer.
■ **PROBLEMS** None.

Caryopteris x *clandonensis* 'Heavenly Blue'

Recommended varieties

C. x *clandonensis* bears clusters of bright blue flowers in late summer and early autumn; the variety 'Heavenly Blue' has a more erect, compact habit and deeper blue flowers; 'Kew Blue' is also compact, with rich blue flowers; 'Worcester Gold' has golden-yellow foliage but at the expense of less attractive flowers.

Cassia Senna

❝ *I've deliberately included a few marginally hardy plants because the summer offers the opportunity of growing such species outdoors in containers and then moving them under cover in the winter. Cassia is one of them although my recommended variety will survive outdoors in sheltered spots. It is popularly known as senna (and is the source of the well known purgative of the same name) and it is in the genus* Senna *that the familiar forms are now often placed. With their characteristic pea family flowers, they are immediately familiar even if few people can name them.* ❞

FLOWERS Clusters of cup-shaped, rich yellow flowers, sometimes fragrant.
PERIOD OF FLOWERING Throughout much of the summer, depending on species.
NON-FLOWERING APPEAL Attractive pinnate evergreen or semi-evergreen foliage.
SITE AND SOIL Needs full sunlight and fertile, well-drained soil.
HARDINESS Barely hardy, tolerating around -5°C (23°F).
SIZE Some species grow to small tree height, but in temperate climates *C. corymbosa* will reach a maximum of about 2 x 2m (6½ x 6½ft).

■ **PRUNING** None essential.
■ **PROPAGATION** Seed in spring or hardwood cuttings in late autumn in a cool greenhouse.
■ **PROBLEMS** None.

Recommended varieties

C. corymbosa from the southern US and temperate South America is the best, bearing sprays of bright yellow flowers in late summer.

Cassia corymbosa

CEANOTHUS

Ceanothus Californian lilac

" *Although I've drawn favourable comparisons between* Caryopteris *and* Ceanothus*, there's no denying that the Californian lilacs are and will remain the more popular. The flowers are individually much smaller (hence the common name, referring to the very similar inflorescences of real lilacs), but the numerous species have hybridised freely to yield some excellent varieties; and of course, there are both evergreen and deciduous types with different flowering times.* "

FLOWERS Masses of tiny, usually blue flowers, sometimes fragrant and in a range of shades from powder blue to very dark; a few types have pink flowers.

PERIOD OF FLOWERING Varies with type; evergreen forms generally flower from spring into early summer; deciduous types from late summer into autumn.

NON-FLOWERING APPEAL Many types are evergreen with fairly small, glossy leaves.

SITE AND SOIL Prefers full sun but tolerates light shade. Requires a good rich, deep soil, not strongly alkaline although slight alkalinity can be tolerated if sequestered iron fertilizer is given in spring.

HARDINESS Most forms are fairly to moderately hardy, tolerating -10°C to -15°C (14 to 5°F).

SIZE The evergreen types on average reach about 2 x 2m (6½ x 6½ft) after five years and 4 x 4m (13 x 13ft) after 10 years. Deciduous forms will attain about three-quarters of this size.

■ **PRUNING** Evergreen forms need not be pruned, but new growth may be encouraged by removing a few three to four-year-old shoots after flowering each year. Deciduous types should be cut back hard in spring to about 4cm (1½in) from the start of the previous year's growth.

Recommended varieties
Evergreen: *C. arboreus*, masses of vivid blue flowers in spring; less hardy, and about one-third taller, the form 'Trewithen Blue', subtly fragrant and darker flowers. 'Autumnal Blue', large panicles of dark blue flowers and is one of the hardiest forms. 'Burkwoodii', somewhat smaller and more tender, has rich blue flowers in late spring and early summer and sporadically into autumn. 'Cascade', more open inflorescences of powder-blue flowers in spring. 'Edinburgh', panicles of mid-blue flowers in spring, olive-green leaves, and is less hardy.

C. griseus 'Yankee Point' bears light blue flowers in mid-spring. *C. impressus*, one of the hardiest forms, has masses of small deep blue flowers and unusual dark green curling, deeply-veined leaves. 'Italian Skies', sky-blue flowers in spring, and is less hardy. 'Puget Blue', long-lasting deep blue flowers during spring and summer. 'Southmead', sky-blue flowers in late spring and early summer, and is slightly less hardy. *C. thyrsiflorus*, one of the hardiest forms, has masses of mid-blue flowers in spring and early summer, and dark green leaves; var. *repens* is an excellent low, spreading

plant with profuse rich blue flowers in mid-spring, and dark green, toothed leaves. *C. x veitchianus*, deep blue flowers in late spring and early summer, and is taller and hardier than average.

Deciduous: *C. x delilieanus* 'Gloire de Versailles', large inflorescences of powder-blue flowers in mid- to late summer. *C. x pallidus* 'Marie Simon', rose-pink flowers in mid- to late summer and purplish veined leaves and is about one-third smaller and rather less hardy; 'Perle Rose', similar but smaller leaves and bears pinkish-red flowers in mid- to late summer.

Top: *Ceanothus* x *delileanus* 'Gloire de Versailles' **Above:** *Ceanothus* x *arboreus* 'Trewithen Blue'

■ **PROPAGATION** Evergreens from semi-ripe cuttings taken in midsummer; deciduous forms from softwood cuttings in summer or hardwood cuttings in late autumn to early winter.

■ **PROBLEMS** The foliage of evergreen species may be browned in winter; early-flowering forms may suffer from frost damage. Leaf chlorosis and scale insects can affect all types.

Ceratostigma Shrubby plumbago

❝ *For my money, this plant has the most glorious blue flowers of any that you can grow. They are of the shade that is variously described as 'electric' or 'kingfisher' blue. It isn't a big plant and, in my experience, it is extremely slow to establish but once content, it will flower for year after year in the most undemanding manner.* ❞

FLOWERS Small, long-lasting gloriously blue flowers.
PERIOD OF FLOWERING Late summer and autumn.
NON-FLOWERING APPEAL Foliage has purple-red veins and turns gloriously and vividly red in autumn while the flowers are still present.
SITE AND SOIL Best in full sun but tolerates light shade. Tolerates most soils but thrives best in one that is deep, rich and free-draining.
HARDINESS Hardy, tolerating -15°C to -20°C (5°F to -4°F).
SIZE *Ceratostigma plumbaginoides* has a low, creeping habit; *C. willmottianum* will reach about 1 x 1m (3 x 3ft) each year after annual pruning.

■ **PRUNING** Cut all shoots back to just above soil level in mid-spring. It's particulary important to leave the dead shoots on over winter for protection against frost.
■ **PROPAGATION** By division or by semi-ripe cuttings in late summer.
■ **PROBLEMS** *C. plumbaginoides* can be invasive once well established.

Recommended varieties
C. plumbaginoides is a creeping plant with small clusters of brilliant blue flowers on reddish stems in late summer and autumn. The more upright *C. willmottianum* also bears bright blue flowers in late summer and autumn, when its leaves turn red.

Ceratostigma willmottianum

CESTRUM

Cestrum

❝ *It takes a good deal to move a hard-bitten television director to horticultural emotion. But I remember* Cestrum parqui *doing just that when I was filming in a garden in southern England many years ago. Gardener my director was not, and yet this quietly beautiful deciduous plant in full fragrant bloom near to the front door of a country house moved him close to serious enthusiasm. I hope it will do the same for even more people after reading this.* ❞

Cestrum parqui

FLOWERS Large, showy flower heads ranging in colour from yellow-green to red.
PERIOD OF FLOWERING Early to late summer, depending on variety.
NON-FLOWERING APPEAL There are some evergreen forms, although they are much less hardy and only for the most sheltered spots.
SITE AND SOIL Needs some support against a sunny sheltered wall or in a conservatory. Tolerant of most well-drained, friable soils.
HARDINESS Barely hardy, tolerating around -5°C (23°F).
SIZE About 1 x 1m (3 x 3ft) after five years; 2 x 2m (6½ x 6½ft) after 10 years.

■ **PRUNING** Cut out the oldest one-third of the shoots in spring each year.
■ **PROPAGATION** Semi-ripe cuttings in midsummer. Maintain warmth with bottom heat in autumn, as a temperature of around 18-21°C (65-70°F) is needed to form roots.
■ **PROBLEMS** May suffer from wind chill or frost damage.

Recommended varieties
C. elegans, evergreen, has clusters of bright red flowers through summer and autumn. 'Newellii' is similar, but has orange-red flowers. *C. parqui*, (the Willow-leaved jessamine) is much the hardiest with yellow-green flowers from early to midsummer that are fragrant at night.

Chaenomeles
Japanese quince

❝ *Yes, you can make the fruit into a type of quince jelly although they have nothing of the flavour or qualities of real quinces* (Cydonia oblonga). *That quite simply is the answer to almost the only question that I am ever asked about the ornamental Japanese quince. I can only assume that this must mean that it is a relatively easy and trouble-free plant for it is grown in thousands of gardens adding a bright, sometimes very bright splash of colour throughout the spring and into early summer.* ❞

Recommended varieties
There are three groups of plants: *C. japonica* from Japan, with few worthy varieties, *C. speciosa*, and *C. x superba*, a hybrid between the two. There are many varieties of which the following are those I know best: *C. speciosa* varieties: 'Geisha Girl' has deep apricot flowers; 'Moerloosei' or 'Apple Blossom' has clusters of pale pink and white flowers; 'Nivalis' has large pure white flowers. *C. x superba* varieties: 'Crimson and Gold' has crimson-petals with golden anthers; 'Knap Hill Scarlet' has profuse orange-scarlet flowers; 'Nicoline' is a very spreading plant, less suitable for wall training, with scarlet flowers; 'Pink Lady' is also spreading, with rose-pink flowers; 'Rowallane' has large blood-red flowers.

Chaenomeles x superba

Choisya Mexican orange blossom

I have an axe that I grind from time to time: I am weary of opening a shrub catalogue to find that some plant that I have known and loved for years has been replaced by a newer form; and that the newer form is no improvement. I become especially irritated when a fine plant with all-green foliage is replaced with a variegated or 'golden' version. And this, sadly, has been the fate of Choisya ternata. Many nurseries do still stock it; but many others have dropped it in favour of 'Sundance', its bilious-looking variant.

FLOWERS Single apple blossom-like flowers in shades of red, pink, white and orange are borne profusely on wood two years old or more.

PERIOD OF FLOWERING Early spring to early summer.

NON-FLOWERING APPEAL Attractive pear-shaped fruits that are fragrant and may be used similarly to true quinces. Some autumn foliage colour.

SITE AND SOIL Best in full sun, but will tolerate some shade. Probably most commonly grown against a wall although not all varieties are equally suitable; many of the varieties derived from the two species (see below) are too lax and persistently grow away from the wall. Thrives in all except very alkaline soils.

HARDINESS Hardy, tolerating around -18°C (0°F).

SIZE *C. japonica* varieties will attain about 1m x 75cm (3ft x 30in); *C. speciosa* varieties about 2 x 2m (6½ x 6½ft) after five years and 3 x 4m (10 x 13ft) after 10 years; *C. x superba* varieties about half this size.

FLOWERS Large, white, orange-scented flowers.

PERIOD OF FLOWERING Late spring to early summer.

NON-FLOWERING APPEAL Evergreen, glossy, rather aromatic foliage of attractive form.

SITE AND SOIL Thrives in sun or shade, but intolerant of exposure. Tolerates all but the most alkaline soils.

HARDINESS Fairly hardy, tolerating around -10°C (14°F).

SIZE *C. ternata* will reach about 2-3m x 2-3m (6½-10 x 6½-10ft) after 10 years; 'Sundance' about two-thirds of this and 'Aztec Pearl' about half.

Recommended varieties
C. ternata is the best form, with glossy dark green foliage; the variety 'Sundance' has the yellowish foliage, especially when young, that I dislike so much; 'Aztec Pearl' has almond-scented flowers flushed with pink.

Choisya ternata

■ **PRUNING** Cut all previous season's growth on wall trained plants back to two buds in early spring before flowering, taking care not to remove flowering buds. Free-standing plants need little or no pruning.

■ **PROPAGATION** Semi-ripe cuttings in midsummer.

■ **PROBLEMS** May suffer from common diseases of the rose family such as canker, fireblight or scab; also leaf chlorosis in alkaline soils.

■ **PRUNING** On mature plants, cut back the oldest one-third of the stems to soil level after flowering each year to encourage new growth.

■ **PROPAGATION** Softwood or semi-ripe cuttings in summer.

■ **PROBLEMS** Old plants may become woody if pruning isn't attended to. All varieties I find often suffer from frost damage or chlorosis, although this is often over looked on the pale leaved 'Sundance'.

Cistus Rock rose

❝ *Don't let the common name rock rose mislead you; these aren't plants for the rock garden, they are too big for that. Certainly in their natural habitat nonetheless, they do thrive on the rocky sun-baked hill sides of the Mediterranean but in gardens, it is warmth and dryness that they require most to produce their striking, generally single flowers.* ❞

FLOWERS Large, flat, single yellow-centred flowers ranging from white to pink and purple and lasting only for a day, with new buds opening in quick succession.

PERIOD OF FLOWERING Throughout the summer.

NON-FLOWERING APPEAL Attractive evergreen foliage that is either green and glossy or grey and downy.

SITE AND SOIL Needs shelter and full sun, so may usefully be grown against a warm wall; tolerates all soils, even if highly alkaline.

HARDINESS Moderately hardy, tolerating -10°C (14°F).

SIZE About 1 x 1m (3 x 3ft) after five years.

■ **PRUNING** On mature plants remove the oldest one-third of shoots to soil level after flowering.
■ **PROPAGATION** Softwood cuttings in early to midsummer.
■ **PROBLEMS** None.

Recommended varieties

Cistus x *aguilarii* 'Maculatus' has white flowers with a central ring of crimson splashes, and green, glossy foliage. *C.* x *cyprius* and *C.* x *dansereaui* 'Decumbens' have white flowers with crimson markings; *C.* x *d.* 'Elma' has pure white flowers, *C.* x *hybridus* is one of the hardiest forms, with white flowers opening from crimson buds. *C. ladanifer* is tall, erect, with white flowers that have dark brown blotches. *C. laurifolius* is tall, probably the hardiest, with white flowers. *C.* x *laxus* 'Snow White' is spreading, with white flowers. *C.* x *pulverulentus* 'Sunset' is dwarf with brilliant cerise flowers; 'Warley Rose' has cerise flowers, and sage-green foliage. *C.* x *purpureus* has deep purple-pink flowers blotched with deep red, and grey-green leaves. 'Silver Pink' is small, hardy, with silver-pink flowers. *C.* x *skanbergii* is small with white-pink flowers *C.* x *stenophyllus* has white flowers with a crimson spot.

Cistus x *purpureus*

Clerodendrum

❝ *The flowers and fruits of clerodendrums are among the most striking of any in the garden. It surprises me that they aren't more frequently grown and I suspect that part of the reason may be that they aren't widely enough stocked. This is probably because they are rather slow to establish and tend to sulk after being moved. But if you can tolerate this foible, the result will be a plant that will turn heads.* ❞

FLOWERS Vary with species. Those of *Clerodendrum bungei* are individually elongated tubular, deep pink, red or purple and in dense inflorescences at the end of the shoots. Those of *C. trichotomum* are slightly larger, and in slightly larger inflorescences, strikingly red with white sepals. All are fragrant.

PERIOD OF FLOWERING Late summer to early autumn.

NON-FLOWERING APPEAL Large heart-shaped leaves and, in some cases, bright blue autumn fruits.

SITE AND SOIL Prefers light shade. Thrives on most soils except those extremely alkaline.

HARDINESS Hardy, tolerating around -10°C (14°F).

SIZE *C. bungei* will reach a maximum of 1 x 2.5m (3 x 8ft); *C. trichotomum* will reach about 1.5 x 1.5m (5 x 5ft) after five years, 3.5 x 3.5m (11 x 11ft) after 15 years and will eventually, in milder areas, make a tree of 6m (20ft) or more.

- **PRUNING** None needed for *C. trichotomum* but *C. bungei* should be cut back to just above soil level in spring to encourage new growth.
- **PROPAGATION** Softwood cuttings in late spring, or semi-ripe cuttings in summer.
- **PROBLEMS** Whiteflies, red spider mites and mealy bugs may be troublesome.

Clerodendrum trichotomum

Recommended varieties

C. bungei can be evergreen or deciduous, with domed clusters of small, fragrant deep pink flowers. *C. trichotomum* is a deciduous large shrub or small tree with clusters of fragrant white flowers opening from deep pink and greenish-white buds, followed by very attractive and unusual blue fruits; var. *fargesii* has very fragrant white flowers and maroon calyces, also followed by bright blue fruits.

Clethra Summer sweet, Pepper bush

" Clethras have always been much commoner in North American than British gardens. Partly this must be because they, or at least some of them, are North American and not European plants; American gardeners can be parochial. But I think it's also because British gardeners have never been very enthusiastic about shrubs whose primary merit is perfume. Perhaps we feel that something so big must have good visual appeal too. Perhaps Clethra *can make some converts. "*

FLOWERS Spice-perfumed, white or pink bell-shaped.
PERIOD OF FLOWERING Late summer to early autumn.
NON-FLOWERING APPEAL Some forms have glossy foliage, some autumn colour, and some have attractive peeling bark.
SITE AND SOIL Needs semi-shade and a moist, lime-free soil.
HARDINESS Hardy, tolerating -15°C (5°F).
SIZE 1 x 1m (3 x 3ft) after five years, 2.5 x 3m (8 x 10ft) after 10 years.

- **PRUNING** None essential, but mature plants may be thinned out to promote new growth.
- **PROPAGATION** Softwood cuttings in summer.
- **PROBLEMS** None.

Recommended varieties

C. alnifolia bears upright panicles of small creamy-white flowers; 'Paniculata' is a smaller form with more abundant flowers; 'Pink Spire' and 'Rosea' are small to medium forms with pink-tinged buds and flowers and glossy leaves.

Clethra alnifolia **'Rosea'**

COLUTEA

Colutea Bladder senna

" I wake up to the sight of a Colutea every morning. Not that it is a house-plant but the subject of an old botanical print that hangs on my bedroom wall. I was attracted to buy it years ago, as I am still, by the remarkably inflated seed pods into which the rather more familiar pea-like flowers develop. Pretty easy to grow, with flowers that are pretty easy on the eye and, with those curious fruits, coluteas should be in more shrub borders; and perhaps more bedrooms too. "

FLOWERS Pea-like yellow or orange flowers.
PERIOD OF FLOWERING Throughout the summer.
NON-FLOWERING APPEAL Attractive pinnate foliage and hugely inflated, bladder-shaped seed pods in late summer and autumn.
SITE AND SOIL Best in full sun; thrives in any but the most water-logged soil.
HARDINESS Hardy, tolerating -15°C (5°F).
SIZE 2 x 2m (6½ x 6½ft) after five years, 3 x 3m (10 x 10ft) after 10 years.

■ **PRUNING** None essential, but may be cut hard back in spring if necessary to reduce size.
■ **PROPAGATION** Seed, or softwood cuttings in summer.
■ **PROBLEMS** Extensive top growth, especially when in fruit, makes the plants prone to wind damage and it makes sense to support it with a stake.

Recommended varieties
C. arborescens has yellow flowers and mid-green foliage. C. x media 'Copper Beauty' is slightly smaller, with bright orange flowers and blue-green leaves.

Colutea arborescens

Convolvulus

" The thought of deliberately planting anything called Convolvulus will strike terror into the heart of most gardeners. But there are bindweeds and there is C. cneorum; the two have little in common except the name and their rather similar flowers. The shrubby convolvulus of the Mediterranean is a charming and non-invasive plant, although tricky to satisfy. "

FLOWERS Large pale pink and white funnel-shaped flowers opening from pink buds.
PERIOD OF FLOWERING Late spring and early summer.
NON-FLOWERING APPEAL Very attractive narrow, silky, silvery leaves; probably closer to a true silver than almost any other shrub.
SITE AND SOIL Best in full sun, with a gritty, very well-drained soil. Quite intolerant of waterlogging or heavy conditions.
HARDINESS Moderately hardy, tolerating -10°C (14°F) but liable to be browned in cold winters.
SIZE Around 50 x 80cm (20 x 32in).

■ **PRUNING** Trim lightly in early spring to encourage strong new foliage and flower growth.
■ **PROPAGATION** Softwood cuttings in late spring or summer.
■ **PROBLEMS** None.

Recommended varieties
Normal species only is available.

Convolvulus cneorum

FLOWERS Star-shaped flowers, or large showy white or pink bracts resembling petals.

PERIOD OF FLOWERING Late spring to early summer.

NON-FLOWERING APPEAL Foliage often takes on brilliant autumn colours and some varieties have extremely attractive variegated leaves.

SITE AND SOIL Prefers light shade, and any but the most exposed site; better in neutral or slightly acidic soils.

HARDINESS Moderately hardy, tolerating -10 to -15°C (14-5°F).

SIZE *C. controversa* will reach 2 x 2m (6½ x 6½ft) after five years and 7 x 6m (23 x 20ft) after 10. *C. florida* and *C. kousa* will reach about 1 x 1m (3 x 3ft) after 5 years and 5 x 5m (16 x 16ft) or more after 10 years.

■ **PRUNING** None essential.
■ **PROPAGATION** Softwood cuttings in midsummer, or layers. *C. controversa* 'Variegata' is best grafted.
■ **PROBLEMS** None.

Recommended varieties

C. controversa has clusters of star-shaped white flowers; the glorious form 'Variegata' has tiered branches of bright green leaves with creamy-white margins, turning yellow in autumn. *C. florida* 'Cherokee Chief' has bracts in deep rose red; 'Rainbow' has white bracts and dark green leaves with gold margins, turning purple in autumn. *C. kousa* has cream-white bracts surrounding purple-green flower clusters, and olive-green foliage that turns brilliant orange-red in autumn; the form *C. chinensis* has slightly larger bracts.

Cornus Dogwood

" *In one form or another, dogwoods are among the most versatile of all woody garden ornamentals. They feature strongly in Book 2 of this series,* Best Foliage Shrubs, *where some glorious variegations are on display, and also in Book 11,* Best Winter Plants *for their quite stunningly coloured bark or winter blooms. To find them among summer-flowering shrubs might be a little more surprising but three species,* Cornus controversa, C. florida *and* C. kousa *do have the most appealing flowers; albeit largely dependant on bracts rather than petals for their effect.* "

Cornus kousa

COTONEASTER

Cotoneaster

❝ *I couldn't garden without cotoneasters, and nor could a great many of my fellow gardeners. I would guess that it is one of the most widely sold of all shrub genera. I would guess, too, that most are sold for the appeal of their fruits and also their foliage; either evergreen and enduring or deciduous and with vivid autumn colours. But you can't have fruit without flowers and most also have masses of tiny blossoms in spring or early summer. In general, the medium or taller forms have the most attractive flowers, especially the evergreens such as* Cotoneaster conspicuus, *whose arching branches are covered in white flowers in early summer,* C. 'Cornubia', *which has white flowers followed by large red fruits,* C. franchetii, *white flowers tinged with pink followed by orange-scarlet fruits, and the much less well-known* C. hylmoei, *one of the most ornamental species, which has pink-tinged flowers and long-lasting berries. See also* Book 2, Best Foliage Shrubs, *for outstanding foliage species.* ❞

SITE AND SOIL Best in full sun, but will also thrive in shade. Most will tolerate atmospheric pollution and almost any soil as long as it is well-drained.
HARDINESS Very hardy, tolerating -20°C (-4°F).
SIZE The medium forms will reach about 1 x 3m (3 x 10ft) eventually; the tallest about 7 x 7m (23 x 23ft).

■ **PRUNING** None essential, but may be cut back hard in early spring if mis-shapen or overgrown.
■ **PROPAGATION** Semi-ripe cuttings in summer or by layering.
■ **PROBLEMS** All forms may suffer from fireblight disease but there is little that can be done beyond cutting out affected branches.

Cotoneaster frigidus 'Cornubia'

Crinodendron hookerianum Lantern tree

❝ *This is one of the shrub glories of South America, introduced to Britain from Chile in 1848 and treasured since in milder gardens with acidic soils. Its rich red lantern flowers, set off against distinctive evergreen foliage are really like nothing else. And I've never believed that it is as tender as used to be claimed. Given shelter, there's many a garden in milder areas that could grow it.* ❞

Crinodendron hookerianum

FLOWERS Deep crimson, lantern-shaped flowers hang in clusters on long stems beneath the mature branches.
PERIOD OF FLOWERING Late spring to midsummer.
NON-FLOWERING APPEAL Dark green evergreen leaves with silvery undersides and an overall stately appearance.

SITE AND SOIL Full sun to light shade and shelter from cold winds; needs acid soil, and is intolerant of any alkalinity.
HARDINESS Moderately hardy, tolerating -10°C (14°F) but browned by cold wind in winter.
SIZE 1m x 80cm (3ft x 32in) after five years, 3 x 1.5m (10 x 5ft) after 10 years.

■ PRUNING None essential.
■ PROPAGATION Softwood cuttings in early summer.
■ PROBLEMS Slow to establish and prone to scorch from cold wind.

Recommended varieties
Normal species only is available. A related plant, *Crinodendron patagua*, is sometimes offered and has more slender white flowers.

Cuphea hyssopifolia False heather

❝ *See a* Cuphea *out of flower and the common name of False heather is immediately understandable, for the foliage could indeed be that of an* Erica. *Even in bloom, and from a distance, the flowers might be mistaken for those of one of the more tender South African Cape heaths. But it is in fact none of these, belonging to a quite different family and originating in Central America and the West Indies. Not surprisingly, it isn't a tough thing, and is too tender for temperate winters; but grow it in containers and slip it indoors when frosts threaten and you will have a plant to treasure.* ❞

FLOWERS Small white, lilac or pink flowers.
PERIOD OF FLOWERING Summer to autumn.
NON-FLOWERING APPEAL Delicate deep green evergreen, *Erica*-like foliage.
SITE AND SOIL Prefers full sun and fertile, well-drained soil or soil-based compost (in containers).
HARDINESS Barely hardy, tolerating 0 to -5°C (32-23°F).
SIZE 75 x 75cm (30 x 30in).

■ PRUNING Remove old flower-bearing shoots after flowering to encourage bushy growth.
■ PROPAGATION Seed or softwood cuttings in spring or summer.
■ PROBLEMS Tends to be susceptible to red spider mites.

Recommended varieties
C. hyssopifolia is much the commonest species and overall the best for temperate conditions.

Cuphea hyssopifolia

CYTISUS

Cytisus Broom

❝ *Brooms, I think, are a bit out of favour. And this applies to the* Genista *and* Spartium *(page 46 and 86) species as well as to those in* Cytisus. *Perhaps it is simply that more 'fashionable' things have come along, although the fact that relatively few new broom varieties have been developed in recent years also has something to with it. Nurseries and garden centres seem obsessed with the new and tend, therefore, to forget the old. I shan't make this mistake and commend to you a group of plants that to me are perfectly redolent of warm days. Some are for spring only but those I suggest here will reliably flower well into the summer.* ❞

FLOWERS Prolific pea-like flowers, sometimes fragrant.
PERIOD OF FLOWERING Early to midsummer.
NON-FLOWERING APPEAL
C. battandieri has very attractive delicate silvery-grey foliage and can create a stunning feature when trained fairly formally against a wall.
SITE AND SOIL Best in full sun: *C. battandieri* is often grown as a wall shrub and thrives on most soils except very shallow chalky types. *C. multiflora* is better in neutral or slightly acid soil.
HARDINESS Fairly hardy to hardy, tolerating -10 to -15°C (14-5°F).
SIZE *C. battandieri* will attain about 3.5 x 3.5m (11 x 11ft) after five years, 7 x 7m (23 x 23ft) after 10 years. *C. multiflorus* will attain about half this size.

■ **PRUNING** None essential although *C. battandieri* may be espalier trained very effectively. If necessary to restrict size, cut back young wood after flowering. Cutting into old wood may cause die-back.

■ **PROPAGATION** Semi-ripe cuttings in early to midsummer.
■ **PROBLEMS** All species tend to be rather short lived and may die suddenly and apparently without reason.

Cytisus battandieri

Recommended varieties
C. battandieri (sometimes, sad to relate, listed as *Argyrocytisus*) (Moroccan or Pineapple Broom), has bright yellow pineapple-scented flowers. *C. multiflorus* (White Spanish broom), has pure white flowers all along its branches.

Daboecia Irish heath

❝ *I have always been inclined to think of* Daboecia *as the forgotten heather.* Calluna *and* Erica *are extremely well known and grow in thousands of gardens.* Daboecia *isn't, and yet has the finest flowers of any of them. As its common name suggests, it is in fact an Irish, not a British species. Like the strawberry tree,* Arbutus, *it has a strange distribution along the western side of southern Europe and extends northwards to western Ireland. I maintain that it really should be alongside its better known relatives in every garden that can grow them.* ❞

FLOWERS Long-lasting, small, pendent, vase-shaped, white, pink or purple.
PERIOD OF FLOWERING Early summer to late autumn.
NON-FLOWERING APPEAL
Evergreen, small purple-green glossy leaves that are silver underneath. May bear small brown seedheads in winter.
SITE AND SOIL Prefers light shade, and must have neutral or, better, acid soil.
HARDINESS Very hardy, tolerating -20°C (-4°F), but foliage may be damaged by wind chill and is always better in milder areas.
SIZE 20 x 60cm (8 x 24in) after five years, 20cm x 1m (8in x 3ft) after 10 years.

- **PRUNING** Trim lightly with shears in early spring.
- **PROPAGATION** Softwood cuttings in early summer.
- **PROBLEMS** None.

Recommended varieties
D. cantabrica (Irish or Connemara heath), has clusters of large rose-purple flowers on upright flower spikes. Although there are fewer varieties than in *Erica*, there is still a wide range: 'Alba' has white flowers; 'Atropurpurea' has dark rose purple flowers; 'Bicolor' has striped white and rose-purple flowers, not to everyone's taste; 'David Moss' has white flowers with glossy dark green foliage; 'Praegerae' has deep rich purple flowers; 'Waley's Red' has blue-tinged magenta flowers. *D. x scotica* is probably a hybrid with *D. azorica* and its varieties include 'Jack Drake' with ruby-red flowers and 'William Buchanan' which is taller with deep purple flowers.

Daboecia cantabrica

Daphne

❝ *Daphnes attain their most familiar role as fragrant plants for the winter (see Book 11, Best Winter Plants) but to think of them only in this way is to overlook the fact that several very appealing species have their flowering period from spring and well into the summer. Almost all have the added virtue of attractive fruits and ease of cultivation. Daphnes are among the easiest shrubs to care for.* ❞

FLOWERS Varies widely between species. Clusters of usually pale pink or white, very fragrant flowers borne at the tip of each branch or in clusters close to the leaves.
PERIOD OF FLOWERING Late spring to early summer.
NON-FLOWERING APPEAL Attractive grey-green foliage is semi-evergreen and may take on yellow autumn colour.
SITE AND SOIL Best in light shade and a neutral to acid deep, rich and moist soil.
HARDINESS Fairly hardy, tolerating -5 to -10°C (23-14°F).
SIZE The plants recommended will attain about 60 x 50cm (24 x 20in) after five years, 1 x 1m (3 x 3ft) after 10 years.

- **PRUNING** None essential and may encourage shoot die-back.
- **PROPAGATION** Semi-ripe cuttings in late summer.
- **PROBLEMS** None.

Recommended varieties
Of several daphnes that will flower beyond spring and into the summer, much the best is *D. x burkwoodii*, a hybrid between *D. caucasica* and *D. cneorum*. The best of several varieties are 'Astrid' and 'Somerset', which have larger flowers than the species. There are forms with variegated foliage that I find distinctly unappealing, the foliage merely detracting from the beauty of the flowers. Other species may flower into early summer. *D. acutiloba* has green-white flowers. *D. giraldii* has pale pink to white flowers. *D. x napolitana* has rose-mauve flowers. The lovely evergreen *D. tangutica* has deep mauve flowers, and consistently flowers for long periods in my own garden.

Daphne x burkwoodii 'Somerset'

DESFONTAINEA

Desfontainea

6 6 *Another of those wonderful South American shrubs and, like several others, belonging to a one-species genus. At first sight and out of flower,* Desfontainea *could too easily be dismissed as a none-too-interesting holly. But once those individual flowers open, gardeners everywhere will queue for a view. My only regret is that my own garden offers neither the soil nor the climate for it to perform as it should.* 9 9

FLOWERS Brilliant red tubular flowers tinged with yellow.
PERIOD OF FLOWERING Midsummer.
NON-FLOWERING APPEAL Dark green, glossy, spiny and remarkably holly-like evergreen foliage.
SITE AND SOIL Prefers light to medium shade and an acid, well-drained soil that is deep and rich.
HARDINESS Fairly hardy, tolerating -5 to -10°C (23-14°F), but ideally needs shelter from cold winds.
SIZE 50 x 60cm (20 x 24in) after five years, 1.8 x 1.2m (6 x 4ft) after 10 years.

■ **PRUNING** None essential. Remove frost damaged shoots in Spring.
■ **PROPAGATION** Semi-ripe cuttings in midsummer.
■ **PROBLEMS** May be slow to establish.

Recommended varieties
The species, *D. spinosa* has scarlet flowers about 4cm (1½in) long; 'Harold Comber' has flowers that vary from deep red to vermilion.

Desfontainea spinosa

Desmodium

6 6 *Considering the size of the genus (over 300 species), it's surprising that* Desmodium *is among the many members of the pea family that is ignored by a good many gardeners. Some species are very tender and many are merely perennials, although some are trees, but it is a very variable genus and one shrub in particular makes a good and useful addition to the mixed border for late summer.* 9 9

FLOWERS Small groups of rich deep pink pea-like flowers at the shoot tips.
PERIOD OF FLOWERING Late summer to mid-autumn.
NON-FLOWERING APPEAL Lush, typically pea-like, three lobed mid-green leaves; very interesting flattened seed pods appear in autumn.
SITE AND SOIL Full sun and well-drained soil.
HARDINESS Hardy, tolerating around -15°C (5°F)
SIZE Will attain its full size of around 1.5 x 1m (5 x 3ft) after five years.

■ **PRUNING** None essential.
■ **PROPAGATION** Softwood cuttings in late spring.
■ **PROBLEMS** None.

Recommended varieties
D. elegans is the best of the species likely to be available.

Deutzia

❝ *I see more and more of deutzias in gardens every year, and with good reason for they are very free-flowering, easy to grow and available, it seems, in an increasing range of varieties. They are rather closely related to hydrangeas although their flowers are generally more reminiscent of those of an unrelated genus,* Kalmia. *Indeed, the name of one of the most popular forms,* Deutzia x kalmiflora, *acknowledges this.* ❞

FLOWERS Very small clusters of more-or-less bell-shaped flowers in various shades of white, pink or mauve.

PERIOD OF FLOWERING Late spring to early summer.

NON-FLOWERING APPEAL Olive-green foliage turns yellow or purple in autumn.

SITE AND SOIL Thrive best in full sun or light shade; needs a moist, fairly rich soil and tolerates high alkalinity.

HARDINESS Very hardy, tolerating at least -20°C (-4°F).

SIZE 2 x 1m (6½ x 3ft) after five years, 4 x 3m (13 x 10ft) after 10 years.

■ **PRUNING** Cut back the oldest one-third of the flowering shoots to soil level after flowering.

■ **PROPAGATION** Semi-ripe cuttings in early or midsummer.

■ **PROBLEMS** None, although leaf attacking insects can be troublesome.

Recommended varieties

D. compacta 'Lavender Time' has lilac to pale lavender flowers. *D.* x *elegantissima* has fragrant rose-pink flowers; 'Rosealind' has deep carmine flowers. *D. gracilis* has white flowers. *D.* x *hybrida* 'Magicien' has large, mauve-pink flowers edged with white. 'Mont Rose' has prolific clusters of rose-pink flowers with darker tints. 'Rosea Plena' has double, rose-pink flowers. *D.* x *kalmiflora* has large white flowers tinged with carmine, reminiscent of *Kalmia*. *D.* x *magnifica* has large clusters of double white flowers. *D. monbeigii* has prolific white star-shaped flowers in late summer. *D.* x *rosea* 'Carminea' has rose-carmine flowers flushed with paler pink. *D. scabra* 'Pride of Rochester' has double white flowers. *D. setchuenensis corymbiflora* has domed heads of small white star-shaped flowers and is a truly beautiful though sadly scarce plant.

Deutzia x elegantissima

DIPELTA

Dipelta floribunda

66 *Mention* Dipelta *in a gardening group and I would wager that not one in 10 people would know the plant in question. Why? I'm not really sure except that it is a plant that is, perhaps, rather too much like other things, it isn't so very different from* Kalmia *and* Deutzia *for instance. In its favour are very attractive flowers, tolerance of a fairly wide range of soils (acidity not essential) and rather good autumn foliage colour.* 99

FLOWERS Large, fragrant, pale pink bell-shaped flowers with yellow throats.
PERIOD OF FLOWERING Late spring to early summer.
NON-FLOWERING APPEAL Attractive, peeling, pale brown bark on mature plants and rather good yellow autumn leaf colours.

SITE AND SOIL Best in light shade, but will tolerate medium shade or full sun. Thrives on all but the most alkaline soils.
HARDINESS Very hardy, tolerating -20°C (14°F).
SIZE 2 x 1m (6½ x 3ft) after five years, 4 x 2m (13 x 6½ft) after 10 years.

Recommended varieties
Normal species only is likely to be available.

■ **PRUNING** On established plants, remove the oldest one-quarter to one-third of the flowering shoots after flowering by cutting back to soil level.
■ **PROPAGATION** Semi-ripe cuttings in mid- to late summer although hardwood cuttings in winter may also be successful.
■ **PROBLEMS** Aphids.

Dipelta floribunda

Enkianthus

66 *Anyone with acidic soils will be all too familiar with the family* Ericaceae. *Indeed, I'm sure that there's many an ornamental garden on acid soil where members of this family outnumber others by around 10 to one. But among the ericas, callunas, rhododendrons and others, there's very often no place for* Enkianthus, *an extremely useful rather than outstandingly beautiful plant. It's among the unsung heroes of its family and should be seen much more.* 99

FLOWERS Masses of small, bell- or urn-shaped, yellow-cream flowers with reddish tips.
PERIOD OF FLOWERING Mid-spring to early summer.
NON-FLOWERING APPEAL Attractive grey-green foliage turns bright red and yellow in autumn. Makes a good screening plant.
SITE AND SOIL Best in light shade, and a rich, deep, moisture retentive acid soil.
HARDINESS Very hardy, tolerating -20°C (14°F).
SIZE 1.5 x 1m (5 x 3ft) after five years, 3 x 3m (10 x 10ft) after 10 years.

■ **PRUNING** None essential, but on mature plants one or two old shoots may be cut back to soil level each year to stimulate new growth.
■ **PROPAGATION** Semi-ripe cuttings in summer, seed or by layering.
■ **PROBLEMS** None.

Enkianthus campanulatus

Recommended varieties
Normal species only is most likely to be available, although the related species *E. cernuus* (with a very good deep red-flowered form *rubens*) may also be seen. Other species tend to be earlier, spring flowering only.

Erica
Heather, Heath

❝ Erica *is among the few shrub genera of which I can truly say 'too well known to need describing'. Suffice it to say that the flowers are more showy than those of the related* Calluna *and that there are some varieties tolerant of alkaline soils. These however are of little summer interest and feature in* Book 11, Best Winter Plants. *The big problem with ericas comes with trying to make a choice from the hundreds available; and, even more frustrating, trying to find a supply of a particular variety having made your selection.* ❞

FLOWERS Masses of small, bell-shaped flowers ranging from white to pink, red and purple.
PERIOD OF FLOWERING Early summer to autumn.
NON-FLOWERING APPEAL Attractive foliage that, in some varieties, changes colour in autumn and winter.
SITE AND SOIL Prefers full sun (a very common mistake is to imagine that ericas are shade tolerant) and a moist, not too rich acidic soil (especially for summer-flowering species).
HARDINESS Hardy to very hardy, tolerating -15°C to -20°C (5°F to -4°F), depending on variety.
SIZE About 50 x 50cm (20 x 20in), though some forms such as *E. vagans* may attain nearly twice this size. Ericas generally need replacing, especially in small garden plantings, after five or six years when they become straggly.

Erica vagans 'Birch Glow'

■ **PRUNING** Trim with shears after flowering.
■ **PROPAGATION** Semi-ripe cuttings in early summer.
■ **PROBLEMS** Often suffers in drought conditions, and from scorch by cold winds.

Recommended varieties
E. ciliaris 'Corfe Castle' has deep pink flowers; 'David McClintock' has pink and white flowers; 'Mrs C. H. Gill' has cherry-red flowers; 'Stoborough' has white flowers. *E. cinerea* 'Alba Minor' is dwarf with white flowers; 'C.D. Eason' has dark red-pink flowers; 'C. G. Best' has salmon-pink flowers; 'Cevennes' is upright, with mauve flowers; 'Golden Hue' has golden foliage that turns red in winter; 'Hookstone White' has large white flowers and bright green foliage; 'Pentreath' has deep red-purple flowers; 'Pink Ice' has deep purple flowers; 'Stephen Davis' has scarlet flowers; 'Velvet Night' has very dark purple flowers. *E. tetralix* 'Alba Mollis' has white flowers and grey foliage; 'Con Underwood' has crimson flowers and grey-green foliage; 'Pink Star' is low-growing with lilac-pink flowers and grey-green foliage. *E. vagans* 'Birch Glow' has rose-pink flowers and bright green foliage; 'Cornish Cream' has cream-white flowers; 'Fiddlestone' has rose-cerise flowers; 'Mrs D. F. Maxwell' is a quite superb plant with deep cerise flowers; 'Valerie Proudley' is dwarf with white flowers and bright yellow foliage.

ERIOGONUM

Eriogonum

❝ *The North American eriogonums span the boundary between herbaceous perennials and shrubs but I am very fond of them and have no hesitation in attempting to bring these attractive members of the polygonum family to a wider audience. They have a number of advantages; most importantly, they are very drought tolerant (several species grow naturally on volcanic debris) and they flower for a very long time. Although they will suffer in cold wet places or cold wet seasons, they are pretty hardy in dry gardens.* ❞

FLOWERS Tiny yellow, white or pink flowers borne in clusters.

PERIOD OF FLOWERING
Summer and, in warm conditions, well into autumn.

NON-FLOWERING APPEAL
Attractive, sometimes evergreen, foliage that may be white or silvery and woolly.

SITE AND SOIL Must have full sun and very well-drained soil.

HARDINESS Varies between species; *Eriogonum umbellatum* is moderately hardy, tolerating around -10°C (14°F). Other forms are less hardy.

SIZE Will attain its maximum size of around 60 x 30cm (24 x 12in) after three or four years.

■ **PRUNING** Frost damaged shoots should be cut out in spring.
■ **PROPAGATION** Seed or semi-ripe cuttings in summer.
■ **PROBLEMS** None.

Recommended varieties
E. umbellatum, the Sulphur Flower, has bright yellow flowers that turn copper as they mature, and bright green evergreen foliage that is white and woolly underneath. Several other species of varying hardiness and variously more or less shrubby are sometime offered, but I still feel *E. umbellatum* is the best.

Escallonia

❝ *One of the commonplace shrubs of seaside gardens; commonplace I always feel to the extent that its beauty really isn't appreciated. Gardeners from inland areas, to whom it is less familiar, tend to see it for the beautiful and versatile plant that it is. It can make a truly lovely hedge. It's worth adding that* Escallonia *is one of the numerous fine garden shrub genera whose origin is not widely known. Most gardeners imagine it is Chinese, but it actually represents yet another example of our indebtedness to Chile.* ❞

Escallonia 'Apple Blossom'

FLOWERS Clusters of bell-shaped flowers in white, pink or red.

PERIOD OF FLOWERING Late spring to early summer.

NON-FLOWERING APPEAL Glossy evergreen foliage with grey undersides; a valuable hedge plant in milder areas and especially valuable near to the sea.

SITE AND SOIL Thrives in full sun or medium shade; tolerates all but the most alkaline soils.

HARDINESS Fairly hardy, tolerating -10°C (14°F). The foliage will be browned in cold winter and, in very severe conditions, the plants can die back but will almost invariably shoot again from the old wood.

SIZE About 2 x 2m (6½ x 6½ft) after five years, 3 x 4m (10 x 13ft) after 10 years.

Recommended varieties
Most of the best forms are hybrids with E. rubra somewhere in their parentage: 'Apple Blossom' has large apple-blossom pink flowers; 'C.F. Ball' has red flowers; 'Donard Radiance' has deep pink flowers and large leaves; 'Edinensis' has carmine-pink flowers and large leaves; 'Iveyi' has large pure white flowers and large, dark green leaves; 'Langleyensis' has small, bright carmine-rose flowers and small leaves; 'Peach Blossom' has large bright pink flowers and large leaves. E. rubra itself, usually seen as the selection 'Crimson Spire', has bright crimson flowers and large dark green leaves.

■ **PRUNING** On mature plants cut back the oldest one-third of the shoots to ground level after flowering to encourage new growth. Clip hedges lightly after flowering.

■ **PROPAGATION** Softwood cuttings in midsummer or semi-ripe cuttings in late summer or early autumn.

■ **PROBLEMS** None, apart from cold weather damage (see above).

Euryops

❝ *South African daisies fill our gardens in the summer, although the annuals outnumber all other types. Daisy family shrubs are rather fewer, mainly because most are not hardy enough. Among the tougher types,* Senecio, *is the best known but its familiarity tends to deny garden space to* Euryops, *a neater and more compact plant.* ❞

■ **PRUNING** None essential.
■ **PROPAGATION** Softwood cuttings in summer.
■ **PROBLEMS** Rust.

Euryops pectinatus

FLOWERS Bright yellow, daisy-like flowerheads.

PERIOD OF FLOWERING Late spring to late summer, depending on variety.

NON-FLOWERING APPEAL Evergreen silver-grey or grey-green, sometimes feathery foliage and a neat, rounded overall form.

SITE AND SOIL Needs full sun and very well-drained soil; a good plant for larger rock gardens.

HARDINESS E. acraeus is moderately hardy, tolerating around -15°C (5°F), but E. chrysanthemoides and E. pectinatus are both barely hardy, tolerating 0 to -5°C (32 to 23°F).

SIZE E. acraeus will attain about 30 x 30cm (12 x 12in), E. pectinatus about 1m x 75cm (3ft x 30in).

Recommended varieties
E. acraeus has masses of bright yellow flowers in late spring and early summer. E. pectinatus has large, single yellow flowers in small clusters in late spring and early summer.

Exochorda

❝ Although one or two species of Exochorda *were in our gardens during the nineteenth century, I often feel that the very best, E. giraldii would have been a plant that our Victorian ancestors would have loved. But it didn't reach us from China until 1907. Then, in the hands of the great nurseryman Lemoine, it was crossed with a relative, E. korolkowii to spawn one of the finest and most floriferous of late spring and early summer-flowering shrubs. 'The Bride' should be planted in every garden. ❞*

Exochorda x macrantha 'The Bride'

FLOWERS Large clusters of exquisite, small, pure white flowers.
PERIOD OF FLOWERING Late spring to early summer.
NON-FLOWERING APPEAL Some autumn foliage colour and a very attractive arching habit.
SITE AND SOIL Best in full sun or light shade; thrives on all but the most alkaline soils.
HARDINESS Very hardy, tolerating -20°C (-4°F).
SIZE About 1.5 x 1.8m (5 x 6ft) after five years, 2.5 x 3m (8 x 10ft) after 10 years.

■ **PRUNING** On mature plants, remove the oldest one-third of the shoots after flowering.
■ **PROPAGATION** Softwood cuttings in early summer or semi-ripe cuttings in late summer. May also be layered.
■ **PROBLEMS** None.

Recommended varieties
E. giraldii var. *wilsonii* has the largest flowers, about 5cm (2in) across.
E. macrantha 'The Bride' is the most beautiful, with masses of smaller flowers that create a stunning effect on their arching branches.

Fremontodendron

❝ Once seen, loved forever is most people's reaction to Fremontodendron. *However, it has an infuriating propensity for becoming well established, and then dying without warning or logical reason. Fortunately, it is easily propagated and fairly fast growing, so losses can swiftly be replaced. But it does always pay to take a few cuttings or layers from your plant to ensure that replacements are readily available. ❞*

FLOWERS Striking bright yellow flowers consisting of saucer-shaped calyx and large stigma and stamens.
PERIOD OF FLOWERING Late spring to late autumn.
NON-FLOWERING APPEAL More or less evergreen, heart-shaped, grey-green foliage.
SITE AND SOIL Does best in full sun but will tolerate light shade; often grown very effectively against a wall. Tolerates any soil, even highly alkaline.
HARDINESS Fairly hardy, tolerating around -10°C (14°F).
SIZE About 3 x 3m (10 x 10ft) after five years, 6 x 6m (20 x 20ft) after 10 years.

■ **PRUNING** None essential, but flowering may be increased and size controlled by cutting back new growth by one-third in early spring.
■ **PROPAGATION** Softwood cuttings in early spring, semi-ripe cuttings in late summer or by layering.
■ **PROBLEMS** May be damaged by severe weather when young. The down from the stems may cause an allergic reaction on the skin or in the eyes.

Fremontodendron 'California Glory'

Fuchsia

❝ *Love them or loathe them (and some people do), fuchsias are an unavoidable part of summer gardening. I can't think of a genus of shrubs that flowers for a longer period; nor one in which there are so many varieties. I find it almost impossible to tell the difference between many of the tender forms, but please don't imagine that fuchsias begin and end with the hanging basket and window box varieties. There are many forms that are hardy in at least some parts of the country and can form part of permanent border plantings.* ❞

FLOWERS Ornate and pendent flowers in shades of red, pink, purple, cream and white.

PERIOD OF FLOWERING Late spring to early autumn.

NON-FLOWERING APPEAL Some forms have variegated or golden foliage.

SITE AND SOIL Prefers full sun, but will tolerate light shade. Any well-drained soil from acid to alkaline.

HARDINESS The hardiest fuchsias will tolerate around -20°C (-4°F), especially if given some protection around the crown but degree of hardiness varies widely and only trial and error will indicate which are most reliable in your own garden.

SIZE Varies considerably; most of those I recommend will attain around 1 x 1m (3 x 3ft) after five years and 1.2 x 1.5m (4 x 5ft) after eight or more but there are exceptions; *Fuchsia* 'Riccartonii' will reach 4m (13ft) in mild, moist places.

■ **PRUNING** Where no winter shoot death occurs, no pruning is needed but where the above ground growth is killed in winter, cut back to soil level in early spring to encourage strong new growth. Don't prune in autumn as the dead shoots provide invaluable frost protection in winter.

■ **PROPAGATION** Softwood cuttings in spring or autumn. You will need cold greenhouse space to overwinter cuttings taken in autumn but, as they strike so readily and grow so quickly, it is better to wait until spring.

■ **PROBLEMS** Whiteflies and aphids can cause some trouble in summer.

Fuchsia 'Riccartonii'

GAULTHERIA

Gaultheria

Gaultherias will never be the stars of the shrub border, in summer or at any other time, but there is a good range of very easy, very reliable varieties that provide effective, generally fairly low-growing cover for anywhere with an acid soil. In practice, Gaultheria as a genus has benefited in recent years by being merged with Pernettya, thereby acquiring several good varieties and also the erstwhile intergeneric hybrid x Gaulnettya.

FLOWERS Small white urn-shaped flowers borne in sprays.
PERIOD OF FLOWERING Late spring to early summer.
NON-FLOWERING APPEAL Evergreen foliage and colourful autumn fruits. Often used very effectively as ground cover.
SITE AND SOIL Prefers medium shade but will tolerate full sun. Must have acid soil.
HARDINESS Moderately hardy to very hardy, tolerating -15°C to below -20°C (14°F to below -4°F).
SIZE About 50cm x 1m (20in x 3ft) after five years, 50cm x 3m (20in x 10ft) after 10 years.

■ **PRUNING** None essential but, if straggly, may be cut back to soil level in early spring and will regenerate.
■ **PROPAGATION** Suckers, layers or by semi-ripe cuttings in late summer.
■ **PROBLEMS** May become invasive. So chop back unwanted suckers.

Recommended varieties

G. cuneata is dwarf with narrow leaves and white fruits that have a strange, antiseptic aroma.
G. miqueliana is dwarf with shiny leaves and white or pink fruits.
G. mucronata (formerly *Pernettya mucronata*) has glossy dark green foliage with red veins and fruits in a range of colours; 'Bell's Seedling' has large dark red fruits; 'Crimsonia' has rich crimson fruits; 'Mulberry Wine' has magenta fruits that later turn purple; 'Pink Pearl' has lilac-pink fruits. *G. procumbens* has dark green leaves and bright red, aromatic fruits. *G. shallon* has pink-white flowers, large, leathery leaves tinged with red-purple, and dark purple fruits. *G. x wisleyensis* (formerly x *Gaulnettya x wisleyensis*) 'Pink Pixie' is dwarf with pink-white flowers and purple-red fruits; 'Wisley Pearl' has dark green leaves and large red fruits.

Gaultheria procumbens

Genista

I've mentioned already, in connection with another genus, Cytisus (page 36) that brooms aren't as popular as once they were. The possible exception to this trend is Genista, for there has been widespread promotion of some of its excellent dwarf forms in recent years; and very good plants they make for small gardens, provided they are sunny. I hope that gardeners who already grow these and have realised their value will now be tempted to try some others. And I do hope that gardeners with room and appropriate conditions will try the tree-sized G. aetnensis. Every large, warm garden with good light soil should have it.

FLOWERS Masses of yellow pea-like flowers.
PERIOD OF FLOWERING Late spring to early summer.
NON-FLOWERING APPEAL Many forms have a graceful, arching habit; some form attractive ground cover.
SITE AND SOIL Full sun. Tolerates most soils but fails miserably in wet conditions.
HARDINESS Moderately hardy to hardy, tolerating -10 to -15°C (14 to 5°F).
SIZE *G. aetnensis*, the largest form, will attain 2.5 x 2.5m (8 x 8ft) after five years and 5 x 5m (16 x 16ft) after 10 years. Most others will attain a maximum height and spread of around 1m (3ft).

■ **PRUNING** Not advisable, as brooms tend to die back afterwards.

■ **PROPAGATION** Softwood cuttings in early summer.

■ **PROBLEMS** A strange gall quite commonly arises, the result of attack by a species of mite but it causes no harm and may be cut out if unsightly.

Genista aetnensis

Recommended varieties

G. aetnensis (Mount Etna broom) has golden-yellow flowers that hang from the branches. *G. hispanica* (Spanish gorse) has light yellow flowers borne at the tips of the shoots. *G. lydia* has golden-yellow flowers that entirely cover the branches. *G. pilosa* 'Goldilocks' is dwarf, with masses of golden flowers borne on short stalks; 'Vancouver Gold' is also low growing, but with cascading flowers. *G. sagittalis delphinensis* has gold-yellow flowers on a prostrate plant with curiously flattened green shoots. *G. tenera* 'Golden Shower' is arching with masses of bright yellow, fragrant flowers. *G. tinctoria* (Dyer's greenweed) is spreading, dwarf, with spires of golden-yellow flowers; 'Flore Pleno' is a double form; 'Royal Gold' has profuse single golden flowers.

Grevillea

❝ *Charles Greville was one of the founding fathers of the Royal Horticultural Society and* Grevillea *is his memorial. It belongs to a family little known to temperate European gardeners, the southern hemisphere Proteaceae. They are little known because few are hardy and in this respect,* Grevillea *is no real exception. But the smaller forms do make rather wonderful plants for summer containers, provided they can be given some winter protection.* ❞

Recommended varieties

G. juniperina sulphurea has clusters of small, pale yellow spidery flowers. *G. rosmarinifolia* has clusters of tubular red, pink or white flowers.

Grevillea rosmarinifolia

FLOWERS Spidery, rather long-lasting flowers in shades of red or yellow.

PERIOD OF FLOWERING Spring and summer.

NON-FLOWERING APPEAL Evergreen, dark green needle-like leaves.

SITE AND SOIL Needs full sun and a well-drained, preferably acid soil (or container compost).

HARDINESS Barely hardy, tolerating only 0 to 5°C (32 to 41°F).

SIZE *G. juniperina sulphurea* will grow only to 75 x 75cm (30 x 30in); *G. rosmarinifolia* may attain 2 x 2m (6½ x 6½ft).

■ **PRUNING** None essential.

■ **PROPAGATION** Semi-ripe cuttings in summer.

■ **PROBLEMS** None.

X HALIMIOCISTUS

x *Halimiocistus*

" *Hybrid genera aren't very common; hybrid genera that occur naturally even less so, but crosses between species of* Cistus *and species of* Halimium *do occur in the wild. Others have arisen in cultivation, giving rise to a number of very attractive if rather little-known plants that combine their virtues. Although individually, the flowers are very short lived, collectively they form a stunning display for a very long period; the more plants that can be massed together, the more dramatic the impact.* "

FLOWERS Small, single and elegantly simple white flowers opening in succession over a long period, but individually very short lived.
PERIOD OF FLOWERING Late spring to early autumn.
NON-FLOWERING APPEAL Evergreen grey-green or dark green foliage.
SITE AND SOIL Needs full sun, and thrives on all but the most alkaline soils.
HARDINESS Fairly hardy, tolerating around -10°C (14°F).
SIZE About 40 x 70cm (16 x 28in) after five years, 60cm x 1.2m (24in x 4ft) eventually.

■ **PRUNING** Trim lightly with shears in early spring to encourage strong flowering.
■ **PROPAGATION** Semi-ripe cuttings in midsummer.
■ **PROBLEMS** None.

Recommended varieties
x *Halimiocistus* 'Ingwersenii' is dwarf, spreading, with pure white flowers. x *H. sahucii* has very abundant white flowers. x *H. wintonensis* has pearl-white flowers with crimson and yellow markings in late spring and early summer, and grey-green foliage; 'Merrist Wood Cream' has crimson and yellow markings on cream-yellow flowers.

x Halimiocistus wintonenis

Halimium

" Halimium, *of course, is one parent of x* Halimiocistus, *but most have yellow rather than white flowers. Many plants with names beginning with Hal- are plants of the seashore, since it derives from the Greek for seas and salt. Their seashore origin gives a fair indication of the conditions that they prefer: bright light and free-draining soil.* "

FLOWERS Small to medium sized saucer-shaped flowers, generally in shades of yellow although also white, and often with brown or purple spots towards the base of the petals.
PERIOD OF FLOWERING Late spring to early autumn.
NON-FLOWERING APPEAL Evergreen grey-green foliage.
SITE AND SOIL Needs full sun and a well-drained soil; tolerant of both acidity and alkalinity.
HARDINESS Barely hardy to fairly hardy, tolerating -5 to -10°C (23 to 14°F).
SIZE About 40 x 70cm (16 x 28in) after five years, 60cm x 1.2m (24in x 4ft) ultimately.

■ **PRUNING** Trim lightly with shears in mid-spring to encourage new flowering growth.
■ **PROPAGATION** Semi-ripe cuttings in midsummer.
■ **PROBLEMS** None.

Recommended varieties
H. lasianthum has golden-yellow flowers with dark purple blotches at base of petals. *H. ocymoides* has bright yellow flowers with dark brown markings; *H. umbellatum* is a particularly attractive although less frequently seen species, well worth searching for. It is upright with lovely dark green leaves and white flowers with yellow at the base; 'Susan' is low-growing and spreading with yellow flowers with dark purple centres.

Helianthemum

❝ *Here is yet another relative of* Cistus *and, although more usually called rock roses, the many species and varieties of* Helianthemum *are also, like* Cistus*, known as sun roses. Helianthemums are probably the best known of the group, partly because they have a wider range of flower colours and exist in a greater range of varieties; but also for the very practical reason that they tend to be rather more hardy. You will sometimes find them sold as alpines, which most assuredly they are not; or as herbaceous perennials, which gives a misleading impression of the way they should be grown.* ❞

Helianthemum **'Henfield Brilliant'**

FLOWERS Small, single or double, individually rather short-lived, in a wide range of colours including yellows, oranges, pinks (including some really shocking shades), reds and white.

PERIOD OF FLOWERING Early summer to autumn.

NON-FLOWERING APPEAL Evergreen, greyish green or darker and more glossy foliage.

SITE AND SOIL Full sun and light, free-draining soil.

HARDINESS Moderately hardy, tolerating around -10 to -15°C (14 to 5°F)

SIZE 15-25 x 75cm (6-10 x 30in) after five years; up to 30cm x 1m (12in x 3ft) eventually, depending on variety.

■ **PRUNING** Trim lightly with shears in mid-spring to encourage new flowering growth.
■ **PROPAGATION** Semi-ripe cuttings in midsummer.
■ **PROBLEMS** None.

Recommended varieties
H. 'Amy Baring' has rich golden yellow flowers. 'Fire Dragon' has rich red orange flowers. 'Henfield Brilliant' has deep orange flowers. 'Mrs C.W. Earle' has double scarlet flowers, yellow at the base of the petals. 'Rhodanthe Carneum' has pale pink flowers with an orange centre. 'The Bride' has white flowers with a yellow blotch. 'Wisley Primrose' has pale primrose-yellow flowers.

Hebe

❝ *I was once rather foolish: I said that I would never trust a hebe again; and in doing so, I brought down the wrath of the Hebe Society on to my head. The circumstances arose when, many years ago, I had a small town garden. Pride of place in that garden was taken by two large hebes, of unknown variety, but very pretty; and very prominent. To be honest, much of the garden was constructed around those two plants. Then came a wickedly cold winter, my hebes passed over to where hebes go when they die and my garden had two large holes. But having been spoken to very politely by the hebe people, I gave the genus another chance, concentrating in cold gardens on the tougher types. And I've not regretted it. All originate from the southern hemisphere, many from New Zealand and if you think of them as shrubby veronicas, you will understand why, individually, their flowers look familiar.* ❞

Hebe 'Great Orme'

Hebe salicifolia

FLOWERS More or less elongated spikes or racemes of flowers in white or shades of blue, red or purple.

PERIOD OF FLOWERING Late spring to early autumn.

NON-FLOWERING APPEAL Evergreen foliage that may be light or dark green, purple-green, silver or variegated silver and green. In one very distinctive group, the 'whipcord' varieties, the leaves are much reduced and the whole appearance is very like that of a cypress or similar conifer.

SITE AND SOIL Best in full sun, but the lower-growing varieties will tolerate light shade. All hebes are best in a light, well-drained soil, but tolerate moderate acidity and alkalinity.

HARDINESS Varies considerably between varieties. Those forms with large leaves (and especially reddish-coloured leaves) are barely hardy, tolerating no less than around -5°C (23°F). Those with smaller leaves and especially those that combine small leaves with a low-growing habit are tougher and many will tolerate -15°C (5°F); *Hebe salicifolia* has proved particularly reliable in my own gardens. The whipcord varieties as a group are also reliably hardy.

SIZE Varies widely. The low-growing forms such as *H. pinguifolia* will attain a maximum of about 50cm x 1m (20in x 3ft) after five years. The whipcords will attain a maximum of about 45 x 75cm (18 x 30in) in the same time. The taller forms will attain about 1 x 1m (3 x 3ft) after five years and 1.5 x 3m (5 x 10ft) after 10 years.

■ **PRUNING** Normal leaved varieties may be lightly trimmed in spring to promote new growth. The whipcords should not be pruned and in my experience, they tend to sulk or even die back if they are.

■ **PROPAGATION** Semi-ripe cuttings in summer, or layers.

■ **PROBLEMS** Leaf-spotting can be a serious problem on many of the broad-leaved varieties, also, shoot die-back.

Hebe ochracea 'James Stirling'

Recommended varieties

Low-growing forms: *H. albicans* has small white flowers and rounded, glaucous leaves. 'Autumn Glory' has racemes of deep purple flowers from early summer to late autumn, and dark purple-green, rounded leaves. 'Caledonia' has spikes of violet flowers from spring to autumn and reddish young leaves. 'Emerald Green' has small white flowers in summer and tiny, glossy leaves. *H. macrantha* has short racemes of white flowers in early summer and leathery, bright green leaves. *H. pimeleoides* 'Quicksilver' is a dwarf, spreading plant with pale lilac flowers and tiny silver-blue leaves. *H. pinguifolia* 'Pagei' has spikes of small white flowers in late spring, and glaucous grey-green leaves; a very popular and valuable plant; good in the rock garden. *H. rakaiensis* is very hardy with racemes of white flowers from early to midsummer and small light green leaves. This plant is often described as dwarf and used to be called *H. alpina*, but it isn't dwarf; it forms a huge though magnificent mound of growth. 'Red Edge' has lilac-coloured flowers that become white later, and blue-grey leaves edged with red. 'White Gem' has masses of white flowers in early summer and small, light green leaves. 'Wingletye' has deep mauve leaves in early summer, and small, glaucous leaves. 'Youngii' (also known as 'Carl Teschner') has short racemes of white-throated violet flowers from early to midsummer, and small dark green leaves).

Tall-growing forms: 'Alicia Amherst' has racemes of purple-blue flowers from midsummer into autumn, and glossy dark green leaves. Purple when young. *H. brachysiphon* is one of the hardiest forms, with racemes of white flowers in early summer, and bright green leaves. *H.* x *franciscana* 'Blue Gem' is hardy, with racemes of bright violet-blue flowers throughout the summer and early autumn, and large, mid-green lanceolate leaves. 'Great Orme' has racemes of pink flowers, borne profusely throughout the summer, and light green lanceolate leaves. *H. hulkeana* is more tender but very attractive with clusters of lavender-blue flowers and glossy dark green leaves with red toothed margins. 'La Seduisante' has magenta-purple flowers from early summer to early autumn, and dark green glossy leaves that are flushed with purple when young. 'Marjorie' is very hardy with pale violet and white flowers and rounded mid-green leaves. 'Midsummer Beauty' has lavender flowers and mid- to dark green leaves that are red underneath. 'Mrs Winder' has short bright blue-mauve flowers and bronze-purple leaves with chestnut stems. 'Boughton Silver' is similar but with silvery blue leaves. *H. salicifolia* is very hardy, with short racemes of white flowers throughout the summer, and bright green lanceolate leaves.

Whipcord varieties: *H. cupressoides* has cypress-like green or grey branches, and small pale blue flowers in early to midsummer; *Hebe ochracea* 'James Stirling' is a rounded dwarf form with white flowers.

HIBISCUS

Hibiscus syriacus

❝ The first time that I ever visited the tropics, the first plant that I saw as I stepped off the plane was a hibiscus. And since then, wherever I have been in the tropics, hibiscus, generally in one of the many forms of Hibiscus rosa-sinensis, has been one of the commonest ornamental shrubs. And that sums up most people's perception of Hibiscus as a genus of glorious and very tender tropical plants. But in thinking of them in this way, they miss a great deal, for there are other hibiscus, hardy varieties of H. syriacus, of unknown origin (but probably not Syria) and cultivated in British gardens since the sixteenth century. ❞

FLOWERS Showy trumpet-shaped flowers in white, pink, blue or red, each lasting for a very brief period but appearing in succession over many weeks.
PERIOD OF FLOWERING Late summer to early autumn.
NON-FLOWERING APPEAL Attractive toothed grey-green foliage, sometimes with attractive autumn colour.
SITE AND SOIL Generally best in very light shade but tolerates full sun; must have a light, rich, free-draining soil.
HARDINESS Moderately hardy, tolerating -15°C (5°F), although flower buds may be damaged by late frost.
SIZE About 1 x 1m (3 x 3ft) after five years, 2 x 2m (6½ x 6½ft) after 10 years.

Recommended varieties
H. syriacus 'Diana' has pure white flowers with crimped edges; 'Hamabo' has pale pink flowers with crimson centres; 'Meehanii' is low growing, with lavender flowers and leaves with a yellow margin; 'Oiseau Bleu' (also called 'Bluebird') has violet-blue flowers with darker centres; 'Pink Giant' has pink flowers with deep red centres; 'Red Heart' has white flowers with deep red centres; 'Russian Violet' has bright lilac-pink flowers with deep red centres.

■ **PRUNING** None essential, but on mature plants the previous season's growth may be shortened by up to half to encourage a bushy habit.
■ **PROPAGATION** Semi-ripe cuttings in summer.
■ **PROBLEMS** None.

Hibiscus syriacus 'Oiseau Blue'

Hoheria

❝ Hoherias belong to the same family, the mallow family, as hibiscus. Yet I doubt if more than a handful of gardeners outside New Zealand have ever heard of them. I count this a great pity as they are very beautiful and pretty adaptable too. The best that I have seen have been in coastal gardens but that shouldn't deter gardeners inland from trying them. ❞

FLOWERS Profuse clusters of fragrant white saucer-shaped flowers.
PERIOD OF FLOWERING Mid- to late summer.
NON-FLOWERING APPEAL Very attractive foliage, in some cases evergreen.
SITE AND SOIL Usually best in light shade but will tolerate full sun; needs a deep, rich, light soil, preferably slightly acid, but will tolerate some alkalinity. Needs shelter from very cold winds.
HARDINESS Moderately hardy, tolerating around -10°C (14°F).
SIZE About 2 x 2m (6½ x 6½ft) after five years, 4.5 x 4.5m (15 x 15ft) or more under favourable conditions after 10 years.

■ **PRUNING** None essential, but shoots damaged by winter cold should be cut back in spring.
■ **PROPAGATION** Semi-ripe cuttings in late summer or layers.
■ **PROBLEMS** May suffer damage in severe weather. Can also be prone to coral spot.

Hoheria sexstylosa

Recommended varieties

Hoheria glabrata is deciduous, with white, almost translucent, flowers. *H. lyallii* is deciduous with especially attractive leaves that mature from green to grey. *H. sexstylosa* is evergreen, with glossy narrow leaves. 'Glory of Amlwch' (*H. glabrata* x *H. sexstylosa*) is semi-evergreen with particularly profuse flowers, a very good garden variety.

Holodiscus discolor

❝ *There are many shrubby ornamental plants in the rose family; this is one of the less well known. It is commoner in North American gardens and is a North American species. The flowers are small, even among the blossom trees of the family but strikingly effective for appearing in such huge quantities; from a distance, it could be mistaken for the Russian vine although it won't get out of hand.* ❞

■ **PRUNING** None essential, but on mature plants some of the oldest shoots may be cut back to soil level in spring to encourage new growth.
■ **PROPAGATION** Semi-ripe cuttings in summer, or suckers.
■ **PROBLEMS** None.

FLOWERS Long, pendent, feathery clusters of creamy-white flowers.
PERIOD OF FLOWERING Midsummer.
NON-FLOWERING APPEAL Grey-white leaves that are woolly underneath.
SITE AND SOIL Best in light to medium shade; thrives on any moist soil, whether acid or alkaline, even on heavy clay.
HARDINESS Very hardy, tolerating at least -20°C (-4°F).
SIZE About 2 x 2m (6½ x 6½ft) after five years, 3 x 6m (10 x 20ft) after 10 years.

Recommended varieties
The normal species is the only one likely to be seen although related species are occasionally offered.

Holodiscus discolor

HYDRANGEA

Hydrangea

❝ *Over the years a gardener develops a special affection for certain types of shrub. And hydrangeas are very much among mine, to the extent that I have written standard reference texts on the genus, in spite of the fact that my garden isn't ideal hydrangea territory. I think that all types are at their best in slightly milder, slightly moister places although the common belief that the name hydrangea refers to their love of moisture is incorrect. It refers to the shape of the fruit which resembles an old water vessel. But finally, for anyone who believes that hydrangeas are vulgar blue and pink-flowered things at the seaside, read on and see what you've been missing.* ❞

FLOWERS Large clusters of flowers in white, cream or shades of pink or blue, the latter often depending on the availability in the soil of aluminium, indirectly related to the soil's acidity. In alkaline soils, many pink-flowered 'mop-head' and some 'lace-cap' hydrangeas will turn blue if aluminium sulphate ('bluing powder') is applied to the soil.

PERIOD OF FLOWERING Summer to autumn, with dead flowerheads often remaining attractive into winter.

NON-FLOWERING APPEAL Large, lush foliage, sometimes greyish or purplish, often turning yellow in autumn.

SITE AND SOIL Most forms prefer light shade, and suffer in either full sun or deep shade. Thrives on any good, moist soil; dislikes waterlogging which tends to lead to serious root rot.

HARDINESS Moderately hardy: most forms will tolerate around -15°C (5°F), but some are slightly more tender and many are prone to damage by late frosts.

SIZE *Hydrangea arborescens* and *H. aspera* will attain about 1 x 1.5m (3 x 5ft) after five years and 3 x 3.5m (10 x 11ft) after 10 years; *H. involucrata* and *H. serrata* will attain only about 60 x 60cm (24 x 24in) after five years and 1.2 x 1.2m (4 x 4ft) after 10 years; *H. macrophylla* (and the many mop-head and other varieties derived from it) and *H. quercifolia* will attain about 1 x 1.2m (3 x 4ft) after five years and 2 x 2.5m (6½ x 8ft) or more after 10 years.

Hydrangea aspera 'Villosa'

Hydrangea macrophylla 'Europa'

Hydrangea **'Mariesii Perfecta'**

Hydrangea paniculata **'Grandiflora'**

■ **PRUNING** None essential for most forms, but on mop-head and lace-cap varieties of *H. macrophylla* it is necessary to remove up to one-third of the oldest non-flowered shoots in late spring each year to a few centimetres (about an inch) above soil level, and at the same time remove dead flowerheads, cutting back to a strong pair of leaves. *H. paniculata* should be pruned in mid-spring, cutting back the previous season's growth to within three buds of the base.

■ **PROPAGATION** Semi-ripe cuttings in late summer, but remove all large leaves.

■ **PROBLEMS** Powdery mildew in hot summers; leaves may be attacked by capsid bugs.

Recommended varieties

H. arborescens 'Annabelle' has very large cream-white flowerheads; *H. aspera* 'Villosa' has large lilac-blue lace-cap flowerheads, and hairy stems and foliage, the best of all the lace-cap hydrangeas. *H. involucrata* 'Hortensis' is a very pretty dwarf form with double blue or pink flowers surrounded by paler or white ray-florets.
As I have explained, the flower colours of *H. macrophylla* varieties depend on the chemistry of the soil and where two colours are given, the first relates to acid and the second to alkaline soils. All are mop-head types unless stated: 'Altona' has mid-blue or cherry-pink flowers; 'Ami Pasquier' has purple-red or crimson flowers; 'Ayesha' has grey-lilac or pink flowers; 'Europa' has clear blue or pale pinkish-blue flowers; 'Générale Vicomtesse de Vibraye' has clear blue or pink flowers; 'Geoffrey Chadbund' is a lace-cap with purple or brick red flowers; 'Lanarth White' is a lace-cap, with bright blue or pink flowers and white ray-florets; 'Madame Emile Mouillère' has white flowers with a blue or pink centre; 'Mariesii Perfecta' (also known as 'Blue Wave') is a lace-cap with blue flowers and blue or pink ray-florets; 'Tricolor' is a lace-cap with white or pale pink flowers and variegated green, grey and yellow foliage, 'Veitchii' is a lace-cap, white or pale pink flowers; 'White Wave' is a lace-cap with blue or pink flowers and white ray-florets. *H. paniculata* 'Grandiflora' has huge clusters of white florets that mature to deep pink; 'Kyushu' has similar flowers and glossy dark green leaves. *H. quercifolia* is a magnificent plant with large white flowerheads and huge oak-like leaves that take on rich red autumn colours, worth growing for the foliage alone. *H. serrata* 'Bluebird' has blue flowerheads with sea-blue or reddish purple ray-florets; 'Grayswood' has blue flowerheads with white ray-florets that mature to pink, then crimson.

HYPERICUM

Hypericum
St John's wort

I'm sure that I have been as guilty as anyone in giving this particular dog a bad name. I have, from time to time, roundly condemned Hypericum calycinum *as ugly, invasive and a downright nuisance; and I have mentioned little or no other species by way of compensation. I now retract most of this. It still isn't a shrub for small gardens but there are others in this large genus that will grow well in more limited space.*

Hypericum 'Hidcote'

FLOWERS Profuse cup-shaped golden-yellow flowers.
PERIOD OF FLOWERING Early summer to late autumn.
NON-FLOWERING APPEAL Semi-evergreen foliage, in some cases making attractive groundcover.
SITE AND SOIL Most forms prefer light shade but will tolerate shadier and sunnier spots. *H. calycinum* tolerates deep shade.
HARDINESS *H. calycinum* is very hardy, tolerating below -20°C (-4°F); but the other forms recommended here are only moderately hardy, tolerating around -15°C (5°F).
SIZE *H. calycinum* will attain a maximum height of 60cm (24in), and a spread of about 1m (3ft) after three years, 2m (6½ft) after eight; the other forms will attain about 60 x 60cm (24 x 24in) after five years, 1.2 x 1.2m (4 x 4ft) after 10 years.

■ **PRUNING** *H. calycinum* may be cut back to soil level in spring every other year to encourage new growth. Other forms should have the oldest one-third of the shoots cut back to soil level each year in spring.
■ **PROPAGATION** Semi-ripe cuttings in summer or hardwood cuttings in winter. *H. calycinum* is most readily propagated from suckers.
■ **PROBLEMS** Rust is now rather serious on some forms, including *H. calycinum*.

Recommended varieties
H. 'Hidcote', a hybrid with *H. calycinum* as one parent, is semi-evergreen, and probably the best ornamental form with large flowers from early summer to late autumn. *H. x moserianum* is a dwarf form with yellow flowers and red anthers. *H. olympicum* is dwarf with bright yellow flowers. *H.* 'Rowallane' is a good semi-evergreen hybrid, although less hardy than 'Hidcote', and has rich golden bowl-shaped flowers.

Hyssopus officinalis

Hyssop is one of those many plants that can find a home in the herb garden or the ornamental border. It is also one of the many that cross the boundary between shrubs and herbaceous perennials.

FLOWERS Small, lipped flowers of typically labiate form, usually blue in the true species but with cultivated variants in white and pink.
PERIOD OF FLOWERING Midsummer to early autumn.
NON-FLOWERING APPEAL Aromatic semi-evergreen foliage used in cooking and herbal medicine; usefully grown as low hedging.
SITE AND SOIL Must have full sun and a fertile well-drained soil.
HARDINESS Very hardy, tolerating -20°C (-4°F).
SIZE Will attain its full size of around 60 x 40cm (24 x 16in) within a season.

■ **PRUNING** Cut back hard in spring or, if grown as a hedge, trim lightly.
■ **PROPAGATION** Softwood cuttings in summer or seed of the species; the variants don't all come true.
■ **PROBLEMS** None.

Recommended varieties
Hyssopus officinalis, has blue flowers; *albus* has white flowers; *roseus* has pink flowers; the subspecies *aristatus* is larger with bright green leaves.

Hyssopus officinalis roseus

Indigofera heterantha

❝ *My first encounter with this plant came when I wanted a shrub with rich violet blue flowers; and a name like* Indigofera *seemed a good place to start. In the event, I was partly disappointed because, although it was pretty, the flowers turned out to be pink but I did unearth an interesting story. The name does indeed derive from a connection with indigo but it has nothing to with the flowers. The rich blue dye is extracted from the leaves and stems and at one time, the import of foreign indigo was fiercely opposed by the British woad industry. The use of both natural indigo and woad declined in the late nineteenth century, however, with the development of synthetic alternatives.* ❞

FLOWERS Spikes of small, pea-like, pink-purple flowers.
PERIOD OF FLOWERING Early summer to early autumn.
NON-FLOWERING APPEAL Delicate grey green foliage that turns yellow in autumn, and an attractive arching habit.
SITE AND SOIL Needs full sun or very light shade; often fan-trained against a wall. Thrives on all soils and is especially successful in dry areas.
HARDINESS Fairly hardy, tolerating around -10°C (14°F).
SIZE About 1.2 x 1.5m (4 x 5ft) after five years, 2 x 3.5m (6½ x 11ft) after 10 years.

■ **PRUNING** Cut back stems by two-thirds or more in spring to encourage new growth. In mild areas may be left unpruned.
■ **PROPAGATION** Softwood cuttings in late spring or early summer.
■ **PROBLEMS** New shoots may be very late to appear in spring, so don't be tempted to write it off too soon.

Recommended varieties
There are no named forms of the normal species although related species may sometimes be offered.

Indigofera heterantha

Itea

❝ Itea *is the Greek word for willow and I'm told that the name came to be given to this plant because of its dangling, catkin-like flowers. Now that's a very odd thing because willows have quite different and most untypical, insect-pollinated upright catkins. To be perfectly truthful, the flowers of* Itea *are far more graceful than almost any catkin that I know and, in some ways, have more in common with the tiny pendulous inflorescences of some of the most beautiful of miniature orchids. The two commonest species, one Chinese, one North American, are lovely plants, not the hardiest of shrubs but wonderful choices for appropriate conditions.* ❞

FLOWERS Fragrant dangling inflorescences of cream-white flowers.
PERIOD OF FLOWERING Mid- to late summer.
NON-FLOWERING APPEAL *I. icicifolia* has evergreen holly-like foliage. *I. virginica* is deciduous, with toothed light green leaves that turn red in autumn.
SITE AND SOIL Always best in very light shade; *I. ilicifolia* thrives on any soil, *I. virginica* any but the most alkaline.
HARDINESS *I. ilicifolia* is fairly hardy, tolerating -10°C (14°F); *I. virginica* is moderately hardy, tolerating -15°C (5°F).
SIZE *I. ilicifolia* will attain about 1 x 1m (3 x 3ft) after five years, 3 x 3m (10 x 10ft) after 10 years; *I. virginica* about 2 x 1m (6½ x 3ft) after five years, 6 x 5m (20 x 16ft) after 10 years.

■ **PRUNING** None essential.
■ **PROPAGATION** Semi-ripe cuttings in early summer.
■ **PROBLEMS** None, but frustrating in my experience because they are very slow to establish.

Itea ilicifolia

Recommended varieties
I. ilicifolia has long catkin-like inflorescence of greenish-white flowers, ageing to yellow. *I. virginica* has upright, creamy-white racemes.

Kalmia

❝ *Kalmias have become very popular, mainly because one or two new and fine forms have arrived in Europe from North America. Indeed, North America is the home of this genus which belongs in the same family, Ericaceae, as so many other lovely flowering shrubs. They are obviously related to rhododendrons and can be thought of as the equivalent in the woodlands of the eastern United States.* ❞

FLOWERS Beautiful saucer- or bell-shaped flowers in shades of pink.
PERIOD OF FLOWERING Mid-spring to early summer.
NON-FLOWERING APPEAL Evergreen, dark green leaves, often with attractive purple veins.
SITE AND SOIL Best in light shade, although it will tolerate full sun but must have a deep, rich, moist acid soil.
HARDINESS Very hardy, tolerating -20°C (-4°F).
SIZE *Kalmia angustifolia* will attain only about 60 x 60cm (24 x 24in) after five years, 1 x 1.2m (3 x 4ft) eventually. Other forms will attain about 1.5 x 1.5m (5 x 5ft) after five years, 3 x 3m (10 x 10ft) after 10 years or more.

Kerria Jew's mallow

Kalmia latifolia

"We never grew Kerria *in the garden when I was a child but a friend's father had a vast thicket of it and it was extremely useful for hiding among when playing adventure games. I've put things right since, and have grown the plant in all of my gardens as it has a very individual charm. It's rather like a golden flowered raspberry cane although why Jew's mallow, I don't know as it is Chinese and belongs to the rose family. Its name, nonetheless, commemorates the celebrated Scottish plant collector and gardener William Kerr."*

- **PRUNING** None essential.
- **PROPAGATION** Layers, or softwood cuttings in summer.
- **PROBLEMS** *K. latifolia* won't flower until very well established.

Recommended varieties
K. angustifolia (Sheep laurel) has rose-red flowers. *K. latifolia* (Calico bush) has bright pink flowers that open from deeper pink buds; the two best forms are 'Olympic Fire' which has vivid red flowers and markedly wavy leaves and 'Ostbo Red' has rich pink flowers that open from bright red buds.

FLOWERS Masses of rich golden-yellow flowers.
PERIOD OF FLOWERING Mid-spring to early summer.
NON-FLOWERING APPEAL Bright green or variegated foliage turning yellow in autumn; attractive green stems in winter and a rather unusual markedly upright habit.
SITE AND SOIL Thrives in full sun to medium shade, and in almost any soil.
HARDINESS Very hardy, tolerating at least -20°C (-4°F).
SIZE About 3 x 1.5m (10 x 5ft) after five years, 3 x 3.5m (10 x 11ft) eventually.

- **PRUNING** Cut back the oldest one-third of the flowering shoots to soil level after flowering.
- **PROPAGATION** Hardwood cuttings in winter, semi-ripe cuttings in summer, or, easiest of all, by removal of rooted suckers.
- **PROBLEMS** None.

Recommended varieties
The single species, *K. japonica* has single, buttercup-shaped flowers; 'Golden Guinea' has very large single flowers; 'Pleniflora' is a more vigorous plant with double flowers and curiously, this was the form first introduced to the West. It wasn't until botanists saw the single-flowered plant some time later that they were able to see in which family it belonged.

Kerria japonica 'Pleniflora'

LAVANDULA

Lavandula Lavender

❝ *Who could possibly garden through the summer without lavender? The characteristic spiky flowerheads have been a part of our gardening for centuries so it comes as a great surprise to many people to realise that no lavender is native to Britain; they originate in the Mediterranean and similar warmer places. Although the range of colours and varieties has surely never been greater, relatively few are truly, reliably hardy in temperate climates. The more tender forms, nonetheless, do make excellent container plants for moving under protection in winter. Look and sniff carefully before making your choice, however, for contrary to what you might imagine, not all lavenders have good fragrance.* ❞

■ **PRUNING** Trim lightly in mid-spring to encourage bushiness, and then prune hard after flowers have faded, for neatness. Lavenders will soon become leggy and untidy if they aren't given this regular attention.

■ **PROPAGATION** Semi-ripe cuttings in summer.

■ **PROBLEMS** Apart from leggy growth through choosing a poor variety or neglecting pruning, the only problems I have found are root rots on wet soil, but these are incurable.

Lavandula 'Hidcote'

Lavandula 'Loddon Pink'

FLOWERS Upright spikes of often very fragrant tiny flowers in shades of blue, mauve, pink or white.

PERIOD OF FLOWERING Mid- to late summer.

NON-FLOWERING APPEAL Attractive grey-green or silvery evergreen foliage.

SITE AND SOIL Must have full sun and a light, well-drained soil.

HARDINESS Varies considerably with variety. Most forms of *Lavandula* x *intermedia* and *L. angustifolia* are very hardy, tolerating around -20°C (-4°F) while *L. stoechas*, *L. dentata*, and *L. viridis* are only fairly hardy, tolerating -5°C (23°F) or sometimes -10°C (14°F).

SIZE Dwarf forms will attain their full size of about 30 x 25cm (12 x 10in) after one year; the tallest about 1m x 75cm (3ft x 30in) after five.

Lavandula stoechas pedunculata

Recommended varieties

The naming of lavender varieties is confusing because many are very similar and botanists just can't decide how many species there are. You will often come across a variety simply called 'Alba', for instance, with no indication of which of the five or so albas it really is. And you will find both 'Nana Alba' and 'Alba Nana', as well as two quite different plants named 'Twickel Purple'. The moral is to buy from a lavender specialist or ensure that you see the plant in flower before buying. The following list uses (as far as I can determine) up-to-date names.

L. 'Alba' has white flowers. *L. angustifolia* (Old English lavender) has mid-blue flowers with silver-grey foliage, among many varieties are: 'Alba' with off-white flowers; 'Folgate' has lavender-blue flowers, later flowering; 'Hidcote' is a superb plant with dense spikes of deep violet-blue flowers; 'Hidcote Pink' has pale pink flowers; 'Imperial Gem' is very similar to 'Hidcote' but rather smaller; 'Loddon Pink' has pink-blue flowers; 'Munstead' has lavender-blue flowers; 'Nana Alba' is dwarf with white flowers and broader leaves; 'Rosea' has lavender-pink flowers; 'Twickel Purple' has purple-blue flowers.

L. dentata has pale lilac flowers with delicate, feathery leaves. *L.* x *intermedia* 'Dutch' is a range of variously coloured hybrids, generally fairly robust; 'Grappenhall' is tall, lax, with lavender-blue flowers; 'Seal' is tall, with pale lavender flowers. *L. lanata* has bright violet flowers and woolly whitish leaves. *L. stoechas* (French lavender) has characteristic bracts protruding from the flower spikes, the true species is dark purple; the form *leucantha* is dwarf with white flowers; *pedunculata* is also dwarf with ear-shaped purple flowers. *L. viridis* has green and white flowers and bright green leaves.

KOLKWITZIA

Kolkwitzia

66 *Many flowering shrubs are undeniably beautiful and* Kolkwitzia *is one of them. Just why it should have been singled out for such special attention by being named 'the beauty bush' is a bit of a mystery, although I was once a passenger in a friend's car when he was so distracted by a kolkwitzia in full flower in someone's garden, that he nearly put us both in a ditch. This head-turning plant is a relative of the honeysuckles but is a one species genus from the mountains of China, introduced to Britain as recently as 1901.* 99

FLOWERS Bell-shaped pink flowers with yellow throats, borne on older wood.
PERIOD OF FLOWERING Late spring to midsummer.
NON-FLOWERING APPEAL Olive- or grey-green foliage with red shading and silver undersides, turning yellow in autumn.
SITE AND SOIL Best in full sun but tolerates light shade; thrives in almost any soil.
HARDINESS Very hardy, tolerating at least -20°C (-4°F).
SIZE About 1.5 x 1.5m (5 x 5ft) after five years, 3 x 3m (10 x 10ft) after 10 years.

■ **PRUNING** Cut back the oldest one-third of the flowering shoots to soil level after flowering.
■ **PROPAGATION** Soft or semi-ripe cuttings in midsummer, or hardwood cuttings in winter.
■ **PROBLEMS** None.

Recommended varieties
The normal species has clusters of pale pink flowers; 'Pink Cloud' has larger flowers in a deeper pink.

Kolkwitzia amabilis

Lavatera
Tree Mallow

66 *There's a good deal of confusion about where shrubs end and herbaceous perennials begin; and it always seems to me that* Lavatera *is really in the middle of the battleground. There are plants here that can almost be classified in one way or the other simply depending on the way that you choose to prune them. But whatever they are called and however they are treated, gardeners seem to love them for their vibrant pinks assault you from gardens up and down the land. Their rightful home nonetheless always seems to be by the sea. They aren't among my favourites; they just aren't subtle enough to be endearing but they are certainly easy, reliable and, yes, colourful.* 99

FLOWERS Large, showy flowers in shades of pink or white, with darker eyes.
PERIOD OF FLOWERING Midsummer to late autumn.
NON-FLOWERING APPEAL Attractive palmate leaves, light or grey-green.
SITE AND SOIL Best in full sun but tolerates light shade. Must have a light, open, free-draining soil. Particularly good in maritime areas.
HARDINESS Fairly hardy, tolerating -5 to -10°C (23 to 14°F).
SIZE About 2.5 x 2m (8 x 6½ft) after five years if unpruned; 1.5-2 x 1.5m (5-6½ x 5ft) each year if pruned hard.

■ **PRUNING** In spring, either cut back all shoots to about 30cm (12in) above soil level, or cut back one-third of shoots to soil level and the rest to about 30cm (12in) below any frost damage.

■ **PROPAGATION** Semi-ripe cuttings in early summer or hardwood cuttings in winter.

■ **PROBLEMS** None.

Recommended varieties

L. 'Barnsley' has very pale pink or even white flowers with red eyes, which may tend to revert to deep pink. 'Blushing Bride' has similar flowers to 'Barnsley' but is less likely to revert. 'Burgundy Wine' has deep purple-pink flowers. *L. maritima* has lilac flowers with purple veins and eyes. 'Pink Frills' has small semi-double pink flowers. 'Rosea' has deep pink flowers. *L. thuringiaca* 'Ice Cool' is a smaller plant with greenish-white flowers.

Lavatera **'Barnsley'**

Ledum

❝ *Ledums aren't common plants in European gardens even though one species,* Ledum palustre *is a British native, albeit a very rare one confined to very acid, boggy situations in the north. They are much more familiar in North America where more species grow and where they have been used for many years by native peoples to produce a drink, commonly known as Labrador tea. No-one will pretend they are the most striking of shrubs but they make very welcome additions to damp, shaded gardens with truly acid soils. They aren't worth trying anywhere else.* ❞

FLOWERS Clusters of small white star-shaped flowers.
PERIOD OF FLOWERING Mid-spring to early summer.
NON-FLOWERING APPEAL Aromatic evergreen foliage.
SITE AND SOIL Best in shade or semi-shade, and a moist, very acidic soil.
HARDINESS Very hardy, tolerating at least -20°C (-4°F).
SIZE *L. groenlandicum* will attain its maximum size of about 80 x 80cm (32 x 32in) after five years; 'Compactum' reaches about half this size.

■ **PRUNING** None, although will improve if dead-headed after flowering.
■ **PROPAGATION** Semi-ripe cuttings in summer or seed in autumn, although I don't think that 'Compactum' comes true.
■ **PROBLEMS** None.

Recommended varieties

L. groenlandicum is the best-known species and the one most likely to be found; 'Compactum' is a dwarf variety.

Ledum groenlandicum

LEPTOSPERMUM

Leptospermum

  " *Leptospermums are truly beautiful plants, closely related to myrtles and, like them, possessed of delightfully fragrant evergreen foliage. Like myrtles too, they are not as hardy as I would wish but in sheltered, warmer and, especially coastal gardens, these predominately Australian and New Zealand plants are well worth trying. Those I've selected are the toughest but you may see other species offered as conservatory plants. If your conservatory is big enough, try them too.* "

Leptospermum scoparium 'Keatleyi'

FLOWERS Masses of small flowers in shades of white, pink and red.
PERIOD OF FLOWERING Early to midsummer.
NON-FLOWERING APPEAL Evergreen purple-green aromatic foliage and reddish stems.
SITE AND SOIL Best in full sun but tolerate light shade; need a moist, rich, neutral to acid soil.
HARDINESS Fairly hardy, tolerating around -10°C (14°F).
SIZE About 2 x 1m (6½ x 3ft) after five years, 4 x 3m (13 x 10ft) after 10 years.

■ **PRUNING** None essential.
■ **PROPAGATION** Semi-ripe cuttings in early to midsummer.
■ **PROBLEMS** None.

Recommended varieties

Leptospermum lanigerum has long silvery leaves that may turn bronze in autumn. *L. myrtifolium* 'Silver Sheen' has silver-grey leaves, reddish stems and later flowers. *L. rupestre* (formerly *L. humifusum*) has leathery leaves that may turn bronze-purple in autumn. *L. scoparium* 'Keatleyi' has large, pale pink flowers and leaves that are crimson when young; 'Nichollsii' has carmine-red flowers and purple-bronze foliage; 'Nichollsii Nanum' is a dwarf version; 'Red Damask' has deep red, double flowers; 'Snow Flurry' has pure white double flowers; *nanum* 'Kiwi' is dwarf with deep pink flowers and bronze foliage.

Leycesteria formosa

  " *This is one of those shrubs that is consistently either spelled or pronounced wrongly. The pronunciation is as in Leicester; the spelling simply an old variant derived from the name of William Leycester (1775-1831), a judge in Bengal and sometime President of the Horticultural Society of India.* "

FLOWERS Large, hanging inflorescences of white flowers contained in wine-red bracts.
PERIOD OF FLOWERING Midsummer to early autumn.
NON-FLOWERING APPEAL Dark or olive-green, red-tinged foliage that turns yellow in autumn; attractive bright green stems in winter; large clusters of purple fruit following the flowers in autumn.
SITE AND SOIL Full sun to medium shade; any soil except the most alkaline or the most dry.
HARDINESS Moderately hardy, tolerating -15°C (-4°F).
SIZE About 2 x 2m (6½ x 6½ft) annually after pruning.

■ **PRUNING** Cut back all shoots to soil level in early to mid-spring to promote vigorous new growth.
■ **PROPAGATION** By division in autumn like a herbaceous perennial or by seed.
■ **PROBLEMS** Fruit are liable to be attacked by insects and the plant is prone to produce a mass of self-sown seedlings.

Leycesteria formosa

Ligustrum Privet

" *The green leaved Japanese privet is one of the most maligned of garden shrubs, especially when used as a hedge; and I freely admit that I've done my own fair share of maligning. The yellow-leaved form is rather pretty as a specimen and the native species is a fairly useful plant when incorporated in an informal hedge of wild plants. But there are other attractive flowering species, both evergreen and deciduous in this rather large and under-appreciated genus.* "

FLOWERS Clusters of white or cream flowers with a musty scent borne on mature wood.

PERIOD OF FLOWERING Mid- to late summer.

NON-FLOWERING APPEAL Some forms are evergreen, some have golden or variegated foliage and some deciduous types offer attractive autumn colour. Clusters of blue-black fruits appear in autumn.

SITE AND SOIL Best in full sun to light or medium shade. Thrives in any soil except very alkaline, very dry, or waterlogged.

HARDINESS Most forms are moderately hardy, tolerating -15°C (5°F); *Ligustrum sinense* is very hardy, tolerating below -20°C (-4°F).

SIZE *L. lucidum* and *L. sinense* will attain about 2 x 2m (6½ x 6½ft) after five years, 8 x 8m (25 x 25ft) after 10 years; the other forms recommended here will attain only half this size.

■ **PRUNING** *L.* 'Vicaryi' should have the current season's growth cut back by at least half in early spring. Other forms need not be pruned, but will quickly regenerate if cut back hard.

■ **PROPAGATION** Semi-ripe cuttings in mid- to late summer, or hardwood cuttings in winter.

■ **PROBLEMS** Aphids.

Recommended varieties

L. lucidum is evergreen, with glossy green leaves, and flowers in late summer; 'Excelsum Superbum' has variegated foliage, edged and mottled with yellow or creamy-white. *L. quihoui* is a beautiful plant, deciduous, flowering profusely in mid- to late summer, with grey or olive-green leaves that turn yellow in autumn. *L. sinense* is deciduous, flowering profusely in midsummer, and with some yellow autumn colouring. *L.* 'Vicaryi' is semi-evergreen, flowering in early to midsummer and with lime-green leaves that mature to gold.

Ligustrum quihoui

LONICERA

Lonicera Honeysuckle

" *Everyone knows the climbing honeysuckles which, more or less attractively and more or less fragrantly, festoon many a garden and cottage; and rather less satisfactorily, many a house pretending to be a cottage. I really don't think they look right anywhere other than in the more casual, informal situation. I'm fairly sure that many people also know* Lonicera nitida *'Baggesen's Gold', a valuable small-leaved evergreen hedging plant, even if they don't immediately make the connection. But I am absolutely certain that far too few people know of the shrubby flowering honeysuckles, although the group includes (admittedly among the slightly more tender forms) some of the most stunning of all summer flowering shrubs. I would love to see them in more gardens.* "

FLOWERS Pairs of flowers in white, yellow or pink, sometimes fragrant, and, in the best forms, arranged in delightful tiered layers.
PERIOD OF FLOWERING Late spring to midsummer.
NON-FLOWERING APPEAL Attractive, long-lasting red or black fruits in autumn; foliage may turn yellow in autumn.
SITE AND SOIL Best in either full sun or light to medium shade; *L. tatarica* is best in light shade. Thrives in almost any soil but needs shelter from cold winds to grow well.
HARDINESS Not straightforward for, although those recommended here will tolerate -15 to -20°C (5 to - 4°F) in winter, some, most notably the lovely *L. maackii* are readily damaged by spring frosts. It is worth giving some protection in late spring.
SIZE Most of the shrubby forms will attain about 1 x 2m (3 x 6½ft) after five years and 3 x 5m (10 x 16ft) after 10 years.

Lonicera involucrata

Recommended varieties

L. involucrata has yellow flowers with red bracts in early summer, followed by shiny black fruits, dark green leaves tinged with purple; var. *ledebourii* has orange-yellow flowers tinged with red. *L. korolkowii* has pink flowers followed by red fruits, and a grey-blue down on stems and foliage. *L. maackii* has tiers of fragrant white flowers that later turn yellow, followed by dark red fruits, a glorious plant when well grown in appropriate conditions. It really should be better known. *L. pyrenaica* has sea-green foliage and larger, funnel-shaped cream and pink flowers in late spring to early summer, followed by orange-red fruits. *L. tatarica* 'Arnold's Red' has rose-pink flowers and large red fruits; 'Hack's Red' has deep pink flowers.

■ **PRUNING** None essential, but up to one-third of the oldest shoots may be cut back to soil level in spring to promote new growth.
■ **PROPAGATION** Semi-ripe cuttings in midsummer, hardwood cuttings in winter or by layering.
■ **PROBLEMS** None.

Lupinus arboreus Tree lupin

" *Everyone knows the herbaceous lupins of summer borders, and some people like them. But their stiffly erect spikes of flowers and often strident bicolours aren't to everyone's taste. Why not then try their shrubby, North American relative with shorter, generally rather more graceful yellow inflorescences but the same deeply divided and characteristic foliage? They are also, in my experience, much less prone to those scourges of the herbaceous border lupin, mildew and aphids.* "

FLOWERS Clusters of fragrant pea-like yellow, or, more rarely, blue or lavender flowers.

PERIOD OF FLOWERING Throughout the summer.

NON-FLOWERING APPEAL Attractive semi-evergreen foliage.

SITE AND SOIL Best in full sun and a well-drained soil.

HARDINESS Moderately hardy, tolerating -10 to -15°C (14 to -4°F).

SIZE Will quickly attain about 2 x 2m (6½ x 6½ft), but tends to be short-lived in some gardens.

- **PRUNING** None essential.
- **PROPAGATION** Seed in autumn.
- **PROBLEMS** None.

Recommended varieties
The normal yellow-flowered species is most likely to be seen although, occasionally blue and mauve-flowered selections are offered.

Lupinus arboreus

Myrtus Myrtle

❝ I've always had a very soft spot for myrtles; and it's become softer with the discovery that some are tougher than I had thought and will survive in my own garden. They combine fragrance of foliage with attractiveness of flower and are among those plants that immediately conjure up their Mediterranean homeland. They have long been a feature of British gardening and since the time of Queen Victoria, sprays of myrtle have traditionally been incorporated into the wedding bouquets of royal brides. ❞

FLOWERS Small, tufted white flowers.

PERIOD OF FLOWERING Midsummer to early autumn.

NON-FLOWERING APPEAL Dark green fragrant evergreen foliage and small purple-black fruits in autumn.

SITE AND SOIL Thrives in full sun to medium shade, and in any well-drained soil.

HARDINESS Most forms of *Myrtus communis* are moderately hardy, tolerating -15°C (-4°F) provided they are sheltered from cold winds and the soil is light and free draining. The glorious *M. luma* is sadly more tender, tolerating at best around -5°C (23°F).

SIZE About 1 x 1m (3 x 3ft) after five years, 4 x 3m (13 x 10ft) after 10 years (in ideal conditions, *M. luma* will grow larger still and makes a fine tree).

- **PRUNING** None essential, but will tolerate cutting back.
- **PROPAGATION** Semi-ripe cuttings in early summer.
- **PROBLEMS** None.

Recommended varieties
M. communis has dense, aromatic foliage; the choice double-flowered variety 'Flore Pleno' is rather rarely seen. *M. luma* (now classified as *Luma apiculata*) is covered in flowers from late summer to early autumn, and has the most beautiful attractive cinnamon-coloured peeling bark, showing a creamy trunk underneath; it is a wonderful plant for a mild, sheltered garden.

Myrtus luma

Neillia

❝ *Neillias are among the lesser-known shrubby members of the rose family. Their flowers are distinctly unlike those of most of their relatives and always remind me of flowering currants. The leaves are rather like currant leaves, too, and it is the overall effect of this rather imposing plant that is its appeal. Why it isn't more widely grown, I'm unsure; it's certainly hardy enough for most gardens and is fairly undemanding in its needs. And it doesn't get blackspot.* ❞

■ **PRUNING** Cut back all of the old flowering shoots to soil level after flowering each year.

■ **PROPAGATION** Semi-ripe cuttings in early summer, by removal of suckers or by layering.

■ **PROBLEMS** None.

FLOWERS Clusters of tubular pink flowers on arching branches.

PERIOD OF FLOWERING Late spring to early summer.

NON-FLOWERING APPEAL Delicate foliage and finely downy stems.

SITE AND SOIL Thrives in full sun to light shade, and in any soil, but dislikes extreme dryness; in its native habitat (western China rather than Tibet), it is a plant of rough streamsides.

HARDINESS Hardy, tolerating -20°C (-4°F).

SIZE About 2 x 2m (6½ x 6½ft) after five years, 2 x 4m (6½ x 13ft) after 10 years.

Recommended varieties

Neillia thibetica is the species most likely to be seen.

Neviusia Alabamensis Alabama snow wreath

❝ *If Neillia is one of the lesser known shrubs in the Rosaceae, Neviusia must be perhaps the least known of all to British gardeners; and yet it is available at a considerable number of nurseries. I hope that this publicity will lead to it becoming more widely available still. It is pretty restricted in its natural habitat, growing on the steep sides of river valleys in Alabama, where it forms a spreading carpet of excellent ground cover, lit up in spring and early summer by the mass of fascinating flowers.* ❞

FLOWERS Unusual cream-white tufted flowers that have no petals, but long stamens.

PERIOD OF FLOWERING Spring to early summer.

NON-FLOWERING APPEAL Arching, spreading habit making excellent ground cover. Although deciduous, the mass of stems is most attractive even in winter.

SITE AND SOIL Best in dappled shade close to trees; thrives in any soil.

HARDINESS Hardy, tolerating -20°C (-4°F).

SIZE About 2 x 2m (6½ x 6½ft) eventually but, for best effect, several should be planted to create a ground-covering mass.

Neillia thibetica

■ **PRUNING** Cut back old and congested growth to soil level after flowering each year.

■ **PROPAGATION** Semi-ripe cuttings in late summer, by removal of suckers, by layering or from seed.

■ **PROBLEMS** None.

Recommended varieties
Species is the only one available.

Olearia **Daisy bush**

❛❛ *Although gardening by the sea has a great many drawbacks, there are some wonderful compensations. I always think that olearias are among them; at least if your garden is near the sea in a reasonably mild area. Olearia is a very big genus, all of its species coming from Australia and New Zealand but most are simply not hardy enough for British gardens, even seaside ones. Those that I've picked out here will do well, however, and as daisy flowered shrubs are at a premium, they should be grown anywhere that is suitable. It's worth saying a word about the shrubby daisies in general for I always find the paucity of hardy species among the extremely frustrating things in gardening. Although there are several tiny flowered types, many of them medicinal herbs, if it's proper rayed daisies that you want, apart from* Olearia, *the best are in* Brachyglottis *(page 19) although a few low growing slightly woody, wiry plants occur also in* Erigeron *and* Felicia. ❜❜

Olearia x macrodonta

FLOWERS Clusters of daisy flowers in white, cream, mauve or blue.
PERIOD OF FLOWERING Midsummer onwards
NON-FLOWERING APPEAL Sea-green or grey-green evergreen foliage with white felted undersides.
SITE AND SOIL Best in full sun, disliking any shade, and in a well-drained, neutral to acid soil. Especially successful in coastal gardens.
HARDINESS Fairly hardy, tolerating around -10°C (14°F).
SIZE About 1 x 1m (3 x 3ft) after five years, 3 x 3m (10 x 10ft) after 10 years.

■ **PRUNING** Cut the oldest one-third of flowering shoots back to soil level after flowering each year. Old and leggy specimens can be rejuvenated by cutting back all of the shoots in the same way, spreading the task over two seasons.

■ **PROPAGATION** Semi-ripe or soft-wood cuttings in early to midsummer.

■ **PROBLEMS** None in a mild climate.

Recommended varieties
O. avicennifolia 'White Confusion' has masses of fragrant white flowers. *O. x haastii* is the commonest form and probably the hardiest, also with masses of white daisy flowers. 'Henry Travers' is a striking plant with lilac flowers with purple centres. *O. ilicifolia* has white flowers and is also reliably hardy. *O. x macrodonta* (New Zealand holly) has sage-green holly-like leaves, and fragrant white flowers.

OZOTHAMNUS

Ozothamnus

❝ My first introduction to Ozothamnus *came in the form of a recommendation from a gardening friend who assured me that it smells of strawberries. On the strength of this, I bought one. It is sweetly aromatic certainly, although I remained unconvinced of strawberries right up to the time that a very cold winter permanently removed all trace of any fragrance, a frustrating problem with this plant. It's a lovely thing, rather in the same category as* Olearia *in being from the southern hemisphere, striking in both flower and foliage, but just too jolly tender for my garden. It would be in the top three of my list of contenders for the best silver in any plant leaf.* ❞

Ozothamnus ledifolius

FLOWERS Small, white fragrant flowers opening from red buds in such profusion that the foliage almost disappears from view.
PERIOD OF FLOWERING Mid- to late summer.
NON-FLOWERING APPEAL Tiny aromatic evergreen leaves that are dark green above, yellow or silver below. Attractive seedheads may also be fragrant.
SITE AND SOIL Best in light shade to full sun, and a well-drained soil.
HARDINESS Barely or fairly hardy, tolerating around -10°C (14°F).
SIZE About 80 x 60cm (32 x 24in) after five years, 1.2 x 1.2m (4 x 4ft) after 10 years.

■ **PRUNING** None essential, but on mature plants one or two shoots may be cut back to soil level each year in spring to encourage new growth.
■ **PROPAGATION** Semi-ripe cuttings in early summer.
■ **PROBLEMS** None.

Recommended varieties
O. ledifolius has yellow shoots and yellow-backed leaves. *O. rosmarinifolius* has curled silver-backed leaves; the variety 'Silver Jubilee' is the best, with silver-grey leaves. Among others seen less frequently but worth trying in mild places are the very dense *O. selago* and the exquisite woolly-leaved *O. coralloides*.

Paeonia Paeony

❝ *If you read plant catalogues, you could be forgiven for thinking that paeonies are either herbaceous perennials or trees. Perennials certainly, herbaceous some, but trees, never. For some reason, the shrub-sized paeonies that don't die back in autumn but retain their woody framework, have become known as tree paeonies, although they seldom exceed 2m (6½ft). I've restricted my description here to one main species and its varieties and also to the so-called Moutan paeonies from China and Japan.* ❞

FLOWERS Showy but short-lived, more-or-less single, cup-shaped flowers in yellow or, alternatively, single to very double and in shades of red, pink, or white.
PERIOD OF FLOWERING Late spring to midsummer.
NON-FLOWERING APPEAL Large, lobed leaves that may turn yellow in autumn; colourful seed pods.
SITE AND SOIL Needs full sun to light shade, and some shelter. Thrives in any but the most alkaline or waterlogged soil; but must not be planted too deeply.
HARDINESS Fairly hardy, tolerating -10°C (14°F).
SIZE Most forms will attain a maximum of about 1.5 x 2m (5 x 6½ft) after 10 or 12 years but, under favourable conditions, *Paeonia delavayi* var. *ludlowii* will eventually become larger still.

Paeonia delavayi

■ **PRUNING** None; and likely to lead to the onset of die-back.

■ **PROPAGATION** *P. delavayi* and its forms will come true from seed and fresh seed germinates readily. Others forms can't be propagated other than by grafting, which isn't easy.

■ **PROBLEMS** A basal die-back of the shoots, common on herbaceous paeonies may affect young or grafted plants of tree paeonies also.

Recommended varieties

P. *delavayi* has blood-red flowers and gold anthers, followed by large fruits with black seeds; var. *lutea* has large, bright yellow cup-shaped flowers; var. *ludlowii* has more golden flowers. P. *suffruticosa* (Moutain paeony) is in many varieties, often with Japanese names and huge white, pink, red or yellow flowers, often double or semi-double, and with maroon or chocolate-brown centres.

Paliurus spina-christi Christ's thorn

❝ *I sometimes think that* Paliurus *has too often been planted for the wrong reason. Its tough, spiny nature has made it a good boundary hedge but such a plant should be put to better use than merely to keep out intruders, for this warm-climate relative of the native buckthorn has very appealing flowers. I always find greenish flowers interesting and I really would like to see this shrub planted more in milder areas, but as an individual shrub, not just a boundary marker.* ❞

FLOWERS Small inflorescences of green-yellow flowers.

PERIOD OF FLOWERING Late summer.

NON-FLOWERING APPEAL Light green toothed leaves that turn yellow in autumn; green-yellow fruits.

SITE AND SOIL Thrives in full sun or light shade, and in most soils if adequately fed.

HARDINESS Fairly hardy, tolerating around -10°C (14°F).

SIZE About 1 x 1m (3 x 3ft) after five years, 4 x 4m (13 x 13ft) after 10 years in favourable localities.

■ **PRUNING** None essential, but will tolerate being cut back in spring to rejuvenate. Hedges may be lightly clipped.

■ **PROPAGATION** Semi-ripe cuttings in late spring or early summer, or layers.

■ **PROBLEMS** Can be slow to establish; patience is a virtue with this plant.

Recommended varieties

Normal species only is available and regrettably, not very widely. But do search and ask for it.

Paliurus spina-christi

PHILADELPHUS

Philadelphus Mock orange

❝ *I have, at the last count, seven different varieties of* Philadelphus *in the garden and some are carefully tucked out of obvious sight. This is a deliberate ploy, because I feel that every garden should have an element of surprise. There is so much pleasure to be derived from walking past a group of shrubs or approaching a corner in the early summer and, just momentarily, being unable to see whence comes that rich, sweet fragrance. They offer among the most entrancing of garden scents and there is a variety for every garden, no matter how large or small. Summer isn't summer until the mock orange has bloomed.* ❞

FLOWERS Fragrant white or cream, single or double flowers.
PERIOD OF FLOWERING Early to midsummer.
NON-FLOWERING APPEAL Some forms have variegated or golden foliage, some take on yellow autumn colours.
SITE AND SOIL Full sun to medium shade, but varieties with golden or variegated foliage will scorch in full sun and cold winds, so should be given dappled shade and shelter. Thrives in any soil, whether acid or alkaline.
HARDINESS Very hardy, tolerating -20°C (-4°F).
SIZE Low-growing varieties such as 'Manteau d'Hermine' will attain about 80 x 80cm (32 x 32in) after five years and 1.2 x 1.2m (4 x 4ft) after 10 years; forms such as 'Belle Etoile', x *lemoinei* and 'Sybille' will attain about 1 x 1m (3 x 3ft) after five years and 1.5 x 1.2m (5 x 4ft) after 10 years; taller forms such as 'Beauclerk', 'Innocence' and 'Virginal' will attain about 1.5 x 1m (5 x 3ft) after five years and 4 x 4m (13 x 13ft) after 10 years.

■ **PRUNING** None essential, but all types will benefit from having the oldest one-third of the shoots cut back to soil level after flowering.
■ **PROPAGATION** Semi-ripe cuttings in summer, hardwood cuttings in winter or, with some varieties, layering.
■ **PROBLEMS** Aphids. Philadelphus seem to have an almost magnetic attraction for the black bean aphids and if the vegetable garden is nearby, they will be a problem.

Philadelphus 'Belle Etoile'

Philadelphus **'Manteau d'Hermine'**

Recommended varieties

P. 'Beauclerk' has large, squarish, single white flowers with pink centres. 'Belle Etoile' has single white flowers with maroon centres. 'Innocence' has single white flowers and sometimes cream-white-variegated foliage. *P.* x *lemoinei* has profuse inflorescences of very fragrant small white flowers. 'Manteau d'Hermine' has very fragrant double cream-white or white flowers. 'Sybille' has squarish, orange-scented, single white flowers that are blotched with purple. 'Virginal' is probably the most popular form, with pure white double flowers covering the branches in midsummer.

Philadelphus **'Virginal'**

PENSTEMON

Penstemon

   " I often think that penstemons are among the forgotten gems of the summer garden. They have been grown for many years and were frequently depicted on the garden illustrations of the nineteenth century. Yet I would guess that not one garden in 10 has them today, which is a pity. I think that part of the blame must lie with the fact that many gardeners don't know how to grow them. They treat them simply as herbaceous perennials and cut them back in the autumn. This is wrong. Think of penstemons as evergreen shrubs, some tall, some short, some creeping, but woody and shrubby nonetheless. Cutting off their tops will seriously weaken them. And even though their above-ground parts may take a battering from cold winds and wet winter weather, it will still provide valuable protection from penetrating cold. Because of their need for winter protection, they do make very good container plants. "

Penstemon heterophyllus purdyi

FLOWERS Funnel-shaped, lipped flowers in a very wide range of colours including shades of red, pink, blue, mauve, orange and white.
PERIOD OF FLOWERING Late spring to late summer.
NON-FLOWERING APPEAL Evergreen or semi-evergreen foliage.
SITE AND SOIL Full sun and very free-draining soil, as in a rock garden.
HARDINESS Not straightforward as although most are hardy or very hardy, tolerating winter minimum temperatures of -15°C (5°F) or below, they are very prone to damage by clinging damp in winter. In areas prone to these conditions, using well ventilated cloches will help them to survive.
SIZE The shrubby forms recommended here are mostly dwarfs that will attain a maximum size of 10-20 x 20-30cm (4-8 x 8-12in).

■ **PRUNING** Lightly trim off dead flowerheads after flowering but do not cut back other top growth before the winter. Damaged shoots can be cut back in mid-spring after the worst of the weather has passed.
■ **PROPAGATION** Softwood or semi-ripe cuttings of non-flowering shoots in midsummer.
■ **PROBLEMS** Eelworm.

Recommended varieties
Penstemon davidsonii var. *menziesii* clusters of lavender-blue flowers and leathery, toothed leaves. *P. fruticosus* var. *scouleri* inflorescences of lavender-blue flowers and narrow leaves; *albus* white flowers. *P. heterophyllus* blue flowers flushed with pink, and grey-green leaves; 'Blue Gem' azure-blue flowers; 'Blue Springs' bright blue flowers. *P. newberryi* deep rose-pink flowers. *P. pinifolius* orange-red flowers and needle-like grey-green leaves. *P. rupicola* deep pink flowers and blue-green leaves.

Perovskia
Russian sage

   " Perovskia is one of those plants for which I have to thank a previous owner of my garden. I had never grown it previously but when clearing an overgrown jungle of what had once been a mixed border, I found it to be one of the few plants worth keeping. Now I wouldn't be without its feathery spires of soft blue in the late summer. It is a colour that mixes particularly well both with silver-grey and with yellow; but as with a number of other plants in the book, don't make the mistake of thinking of it as a herbaceous perennial. "

■ **PRUNING** Cut back completely to soil level each spring to ensure strong new growth.
■ **PROPAGATION** Semi-ripe cuttings in late spring or by division
■ **PROBLEMS** None.

FLOWERS Profuse feathery inflorescences of small lavender-blue flowers.
PERIOD OF FLOWERING Late summer.
NON-FLOWERING APPEAL Aromatic grey-green toothed foliage, turning yellow in autumn.
SITE AND SOIL Requires full sun and a well-drained soil.
HARDINESS Fairly hardy, tolerating around -10°C (14°F).
SIZE Will attain its maximum size of about 80cm x 1m (32in x 3ft) in a season.

Perovskia atriplicifolia **'Blue Spire'**

Recommended varieties
Perovskia atriplicifolia is the most widely available species; the variety 'Blue Spire' has particularly fine, large clusters of lavender-blue flowers and deeply-cut grey-green leaves.

Phygelius

❝ Phygelius *is another of those nineteenth century plants that has made a comeback in recent years through the availability of a range of new colour forms. And it is yet another of those plants that often suffer from not being properly recognised as shrubs. Sometimes known as the Cape figwort, it comes, of course, from South Africa. It needs a little help therefore through a British winter.* ❞

FLOWERS Long, tubular, pendulous flowers in shades of pink, red and orange on rather curious angular branching stems.
PERIOD OF FLOWERING Late summer to early autumn.
NON-FLOWERING APPEAL Usually dark glossy leaves that turn yellow in autumn.
SITE AND SOIL Best in full sun but tolerates light shade; rather effective when grown against a sunny wall. Thrives on most soils provided they are not heavy or waterlogged.
HARDINESS Fairly hardy, tolerating around -10°C (14°F).
SIZE About 1 x 1m (3 x 3ft) after five years, 2 x 2m (6½ x 6½ft) after 10 years in mild areas where growth is not killed back in winter.

■ **PRUNING** In colder areas, cut back to soil level completely in early spring to promote new growth. In milder places or if growing in a very sheltered spot, as against a wall, trim lightly in spring, cutting away damaged shoots.

■ **PROPAGATION** Seed or semi-ripe cuttings in midsummer.
■ **PROBLEMS** None.

Recommended varieties
Phygelius aequalis is less hardy than some, bearing pale dusky pink or red flowers with yellow throats; 'Yellow Trumpet' has pale yellow flowers. *P. capensis* has orange-red or deep red flowers with yellow throats; *coccineus* has large orange-red flowers. *P. x rectus* includes many excellent varieties, such as: 'African Queen' has pale red flowers; 'Devil's Tears' has deep red-pink flowers with orange-red lobes; 'Moonraker' has long, straight, pale yellow flowers; 'Salmon Leap' has orange flowers with orange-red lobes; 'Winchester Fanfare' has dusky red-pink flowers with scarlet lobes.

Phygelius x rectus **'African Queen'**

POTENTILLA

Potentilla fruticosa

❝ *Few plants of the summer garden are as rewarding as potentillas. They flower their hearts out for month after month; and in return for relatively little.* Potentilla *is a large genus but the pretty and rewarding shrubs that I recommend here are all derived from one species,* P. fruticosa, *that occurs widely across the northern hemisphere, including Britain. Never forget, however, that they are plants of the sun and they will sulk miserably in shade and in heavy and wet conditions. Choose your varieties carefully for two reasons: firstly, there is an interesting range in colours, from the soft and subtle to the frankly very assertive; secondly, there is also a considerable range in size from prostrate to tall and rather substantial.* ❞

Potentilla fruticosa 'Goldfinger'

FLOWERS Single, saucer-shaped flowers that may be white, yellow, pink, orange or red.

PERIOD OF FLOWERING Early summer to early autumn.

NON-FLOWERING APPEAL Delicate foliage that may be grey-green or silvery, sometimes giving some yellow autumn colour.

SITE AND SOIL All varieties flower best in full sun although some have their best flower colour in very light shade; they thrive in any soil except those excessively dry, wet or alkaline. They are often thought of as Mediterranean plants and so in need of hot dry slopes. This is wrong. They occur throughout Europe and simply need a sunny position.

HARDINESS Very hardy, tolerating at least -20°C (-4°F) but after a cold winter, the above ground parts look decidedly dead and miserable. Be patient, however, and they will leaf in due course.

SIZE Varies with variety; the low-growing forms will never exceed 25-30cm (10-12in) in height whereas other will attain at least 1.2m (4ft).

■ **PRUNING** None essential, but most varieties benefit from cutting back up to one-third of the oldest shoots to soil level each spring.

■ **PROPAGATION** Semi-ripe cuttings in late summer or hardwood cuttings in winter, but wait until after the worst of the frosts.

■ **PROBLEMS** May come into leaf very late and fool you into thinking that it is dead.

Potentilla fruticosa

Potentilla fruticosa **'Abbotswood'**

PHYSOCARPUS

Physocarpus

" Physocarpus *is one of those genera that achieves its fame almost entirely through one variety of one species: a form of the North American* P.opulifolius *commonly known, because of its peeling bark, as ninebark. It is yet another genus that is not usually recognised as a member of the rose family and is relatively unusual in this family in requiring acidic soil to perform at its best. It's also relatively unusual in the family in being grown primarily for its golden foliage but I find there is more to it than simply the leaves and the flowers really are better than just an added bonus I wish the green leaved species was seen more frequently.* "

FLOWERS Clusters of medium-sized white flowers, usually slightly tinged with pink.

PERIOD OF FLOWERING Early to midsummer.

NON-FLOWERING APPEAL Yellow or golden-yellow foliage. Attractive mahogany-coloured winter stems, with peeling bark.

SITE AND SOIL Best in light shade; the golden foliage tends to scorch in full sun and to turn green in deep shade. Always best in acidic soil although it will tolerate more or less neutral conditions; not successful in most alkaline soil.

HARDINESS Very hardy, tolerating at least -20°C (-4°F).

SIZE About 1.5 x 1.5m (5 x 5ft) after five years, 2.5 x 2.5m (8 x 8ft) after 10 years.

■ **PRUNING** On established plants, cut back the oldest one-third of the flowering shoots to soil level after flowering each year. If this is neglected, the plant not only becomes woody and congested but the leaf colour is poorer too.

■ **PROPAGATION** Semi-ripe cuttings in early summer or hardwood cuttings in winter.

■ **PROBLEMS** None, although, as with most golden foliaged plants, there can be scorching in hot sun.

Recommended varieties
You may occasionally see a better flowering but less hardy species, *P. caotatus* which is well worth trying. *P. opulifolius* 'Dart's Gold' has bright yellow foliage with long-lasting colour and is the best form; 'Luteus' is a good second choice.

Physocarpus opulifolius **'Dart's Gold'**

Piptanthus nepalensis formerly P. laburnifolius

❝ *There are several shrubby members of the pea family, the Leguminosae, with rather similar, and generally yellow flowers. Individually, they are attractive but not really sufficiently distinctive to make them stand out from the crowd, or even to be named with certainty. I feel that* Piptanthus *belongs among them. It's good enough for a large garden but just falls short of earning its keep in a smaller one.* ❞

FLOWERS Short inflorescences of bright yellow laburnum-like flowers.
PERIOD OF FLOWERING Late spring to early summer.
NON-FLOWERING APPEAL Glossy, dark green evergreen foliage, though the older leaves may show some autumn colour before falling. Grey-brown seed-pods in autumn and winter.
SITE AND SOIL Tolerates full sun or moderate shade and makes a successful wall shrub, after the manner of *Cytisus battandieri* (page 36). Thrives in any well-drained soil and tolerant of alkalinity.
HARDINESS Fairly hardy, tolerating around -10°C (14°F), but may lose its leaves in severe winters.
SIZE About 2 x 1.5m (6½ x 5ft) after five years, 4 x 3.5m (13 x 11ft) after 10 years.

Piptanthus nepalensis

■ **PRUNING** On established plants, cut back one or two stems to soil level after flowering to promote new growth.
■ **PROPAGATION** Semi-ripe cuttings in summer, by layering or from seed.
■ **PROBLEMS** None.

> **Recommended varieties**
> The normal species only is available.

Polygala Milkwort

❝ Polygala *is a huge genus of plants of which few are seen in gardens, but there is one low-growing European species that I find utterly charming and which always arouses remark. I grow it in my acid-soil bed although it will survive in neutral soils; I do so because it blends so well with heathers and other plants of the family Ericaceae. I think I can, in all honesty, say that it is one of the most undemanding shrubs that I grow.* ❞

FLOWERS Yellow and purple, rather pea-like flowers.
PERIOD OF FLOWERING *P. chamaebuxus* flowers from mid-spring to early summer; the more tender varieties from spring to early autumn.
NON-FLOWERING APPEAL The hardier forms have leathery, dark green evergreen foliage.
SITE AND SOIL The hardier forms thrive in full sun or partial shade, and need a deep, moist, well-drained soil, not too alkaline. The more tender forms can be grown in containers and moved under cover in less mild areas or simply given cloche protection in winter.
HARDINESS *P. chamaebuxus* is hardy, tolerating around -15°C (5°F). *P. x dalmaisiana* and *P. myrtifolia* are barely hardy, tolerating no less than -5°C (23°F).
SIZE *P. chamaebuxus* is a dwarf species, attaining about 15 x 15cm (6 x 6in); *P. x dalmaisiana* eventually reaches 2 x 1m (6½ x 3ft), *P. myrtifolia* around 1.5 x 1m (5 x 3ft).

■ **PRUNING** None essential.
■ **PROPAGATION** Semi-ripe cuttings in late summer.
■ **PROBLEMS** Whiteflies can be troublesome in hot summers.

> **Recommended varieties**
> *P. chamaebuxus* has cream flowers with yellow tips; var. *grandiflora* is a very good form having bolder, purple flowers with yellow keels. *P. x dalmaisiana* has bright purple flowers. *P. myrtifolia* has green-white flowers with purple veins.

PYRACANTHA

Pyracantha Firethorn

❝ *Although the most outstanding features of pyracanthas are their brilliant autumn fruits, they also bear masses of musty-scented white blossom in early summer which is particularly attractive to bees. They have the familiar glossy, evergreen foliage, sometimes greyish or occasionally, and rather unfortunately, variegated. Pyracanthas are most versatile shrubs which are usually seen trained against a wall, or occasionally used to form a thorny, impenetrable hedge. Much less frequently are they seen free-standing although, both in flower and fruit, they can make a quite stunning impact when grown in this way.* ❞

Recommended varieties
For flowering appeal, I haven't picked out any for special attention as there is little to choose between them but on the assumption that you will appreciate the fruits also, there are a number of fine varieties: P. 'Orange Glow' has masses of orange-red fruits and dark green foliage. P. *rogersiana* thrives in shade and has orange-red fruits; the variety 'Flava', which also thrives in shade has bright yellow fruits.

SITE AND SOIL Most forms tolerate full sun to medium shade, and any but the most alkaline soil.
HARDINESS Very hardy, tolerating at least -20°C (-4°F), although the foliage may be damaged in extreme cold.
SIZE About 2 x 1.2m (6½ x 4ft) after five years, 4 x 3m (13 x 10ft) after 10 years.

■ **PRUNING** None essential, but will tolerate cutting back and shaping (if wall trained) in late winter or early spring. I have to say, nonetheless, that there is no ideal time to prune a pyracantha for whenever you do it, either flower or fruit numbers will suffer.
■ **PROPAGATION** Semi-ripe cuttings in early summer.
■ **PROBLEMS** Fireblight.

Rhodotypos scandens

❝ Rhodotypos *means 'a plant that looks like a rose'. And I suppose if you have a vivid imagination, these large single flowers do have something of a wild rose about them. This plant belongs to the rose family but is the only species in its genus, and a native of China and Japan. In habit, it much more closely resembles its relative* Kerria *and I have seen it described by the name White Jew's mallow. It is easy to grow and undemanding.* ❞

Pyracantha coccinea

FLOWERS Single white flowers 3-4cm (1¼-1½in) across.

PERIOD OF FLOWERING Late spring to early summer.

NON-FLOWERING APPEAL Light green, toothed leaves, shiny black fruits in autumn, attractive, markedly upright green winter stems.

SITE AND SOIL Best in full sun but tolerates light shade; is best in light, free-draining soil, either acid or alkaline.

HARDINESS Very hardy, tolerating at least -20°C (-4°F).

SIZE About 1m x 80cm (3ft x 32in) after five years, 2 x 2m (6½ x 6½ft) after 10 years.

■ **PRUNING** On mature plants cut back the oldest one-third of the flowering stems to soil level after flowering.

■ **PROPAGATION** Semi-ripe cuttings in early summer, or by removal of suckers in autumn.

■ **PROBLEMS** None.

Recommended varieties
Normal species only is available.

Robinia

❝ *For far too many gardeners, the North American genus* Robinia *has come to mean solely the very popular* R. pseudoacacia *'Frisia', a pretty enough golden-foliaged tree. Unfortunately, attention has thereby been diverted from a number of very good and most attractive flowering shrubs or small trees.* ❞

FLOWERS Inflorescences or clusters of white or pink laburnum- or pea-like flowers, sometimes fragrant.

PERIOD OF FLOWERING Late spring to early summer.

NON-FLOWERING APPEAL Attractive pinnate foliage, generally pale or grey-green with yellow autumn colour.

SITE AND SOIL Best in a sheltered site; the flowering forms tend to be better in full sun (which scorches those with pale foliage) thrives on any well-drained soil.

HARDINESS Fairly to moderately hardy, tolerating -10 to -15°C (14 to 5°F).

SIZE Most forms will attain about 3 x 2.5m (10 x 8ft) after five years, and eventually become trees up to 15 x 8m (50 x 25ft), although *R. hispida* itself remains much smaller.

■ **PRUNING** None.

■ **PROPAGATION** Not feasible from cuttings, the hybrids do not come true from seed and suckers are likely to be of *R. pseudoacacia* used as a rootstock.

■ **PROBLEMS** None.

Recommended varieties
R. x *ambigua* 'Bellarosea' has inflorescences of large pink flowers in early summer. *R. hispida* is rather brittle and needs shelter, and has short inflorescences of large, deep pink flowers in late spring and early summer. *R.* x *margaretta* 'Casque Rouge' bears profuse, large, purple-pink flowers. *R. pseudoacacia* has slightly fragrant white flowers with yellow markings, in early summer. *R.* x *slavinii* 'Hillieri' has slightly fragrant lilac-pink flowers in early summer.

Robinia hispida

ROMNEYA

Romneya
Tree poppy

" *Horticulture students tend to make their first acquaintance with* Romneya *as small pieces, about 10cm (4in) long. This is because it offers the classic example of a plant that is propagated by root cuttings. I just hope that the students then take the trouble to grow on their cuttings to full flowering maturity and so make the acquaintance of one of the loveliest of all Californian plants. As befits a plant from a such a warm climate, it requires a little extra care and attention, but those glorious flowers are full enough reward. The only mystery to me is why it should have been named in honour of an Irish astronomer-priest who, as far as I know, wasn't a botanist.* "

FLOWERS Glorious, large, fragrant, poppy-like white flowers with golden stamens.
PERIOD OF FLOWERING Midsummer to mid-autumn.
NON-FLOWERING APPEAL Grey or grey-green foliage turning yellow in autumn.
SITE AND SOIL Needs full sun, and a fairly dry, light soil.
HARDINESS Moderately hardy, tolerating -15°C (5°F), though young plants may be more tender. All will benefit from mulch protection around the crown in winter.
SIZE About 1 x 1m (3 x 3ft) after five years, 1 x 3m (3 x 10ft) after 10 years.

■ **PRUNING** Most shoots will die back to soil level in winter; those that do not should be cut back in early spring.
■ **PROPAGATION** Root cuttings in mid- to late summer.
■ **PROBLEMS** May be hard to establish, but then may become invasive.

Romneya coulteri

Recommended varieties
R. coulteri is the most widely available form; the variety 'White Cloud' has larger flowers and stronger growth.

Rubus
Flowering bramble

" *In common with most gardeners, I've done my fair share of clearing away* Rubus fruticosus *over the years. My present garden was overgrown with brambles and sundry other weedy growth when first I acquired it. This is the classic example of a plant that, in the right place, the wild hedgerows and woodlands, is a wholesome thing, its fruits to be collected with pleasure in the autumn. But in the garden, it's generally an altogether unwelcome resident. Sadly, this state of affairs tends to blind gardeners to the existence of other species in this large and botanically complex genus. Some have good ground-covering foliage but a few also make fine plants worth growing for their summer blossom too. I hope I can create some converts.* "

■ **PRUNING** In wilder gardens, all may be left pretty well to their own devices when they will form a large but attractive tangle. For a more disciplined effect, cut back the oldest one-third of the flowering stems to soil level after flowering. Wear appropriate gloves and other clothing, as most full-grown brambles, of almost every species are very thorny.
■ **PROPAGATION** Semi-ripe cuttings in early summer, shoot tip cuttings in autumn, layering (natural layers can often be found) or by the removal of suckers.
■ **PROBLEMS** Rust, mildew, insect damage.

Rubus x fraseri

FLOWERS Single or occasionally double white, pink or purple-pink flowers.

PERIOD OF FLOWERING Mid- to late summer.

NON-FLOWERING APPEAL Light or mid-green foliage, turning yellow in autumn; attractive, sometimes peeling, red-brown winter stems; in some cases edible fruits.

SITE AND SOIL Best in medium shade, but tolerates full sun to deep shade; will thrive in any except the very driest soil.

HARDINESS Very hardy, tolerating at least -20°C (-4°F).

SIZE Varies with species but on average, about 1 x 1m (3 x 3ft) after five years, 3 x 3m (10 x 10ft) or more after 10 years.

Recommended varieties

R. 'Benenden' is thornless with peeling stems and pure white flowers with golden stamens in late spring. R. x fraseri has fragrant pink flowers from early to late summer. R. nepalensis is a dwarf, creeping evergreen with bristly stems and white flowers followed by edible fruits. R. odoratus has thornless, peeling stems and clusters of fragrant, purple-pink flowers from early summer to early autumn, followed by edible red fruits. R. ulmifolius 'Bellidiflorus' is a quite superb vigorous, rambling shrub, if you have the room for it, with large clusters of double pink flowers in mid-to late summer, and plum-coloured stems.

Salvia Sage

❝ Yes, this is the same genus as the vivid scarlet 'guardsman' annuals so beloved of many growers of bedding plants. They are derived from the tender Brazilian Salvia splendens, *but this important genus of around 900 species also embraces many herbaceous perennials, woody herbs and small shrubs, mainly from Mexico and few of which are widely grown. They represent yet another group of plants that spans the boundary between woody perennial and true shrub. ❞*

FLOWERS Clusters or inflorescences of flowers in bright reds, purples and pinks.

PERIOD OF FLOWERING Late spring to autumn.

NON-FLOWERING APPEAL Deciduous grey-green, sometimes downy leaves.

SITE AND SOIL Needs full sun and a well-drained soil, tolerating either acid or alkaline conditions.

HARDINESS Fairly hardy, tolerating around -10°C (14°F) but all benefit from mulch protection around the crown in winter.

SIZE About 80cm x 1m (32in x 3ft) after five years, 1 x 1.2m (3 x 4ft) after 10 years.

■ **PRUNING** In spring, cut back last season's growth by half, to prevent the plant becoming straggly.

■ **PROPAGATION** Softwood cuttings in midsummer.

■ **PROBLEMS** None.

Recommended varieties

S. fulgens has clusters of large, scarlet, hairy flowers in late summer. S. gesneriiflora has very large scarlet flowers. S. guaranitica has inflorescences of intense blue flowers in summer and autumn; selected colour forms are sometimes grown as annuals. S. involucrata has spikes of sticky magenta flowers from late summer to autumn. S. lavandulifolia is a dwarf with inflorescences of violet flowers in early summer.

Salvia guaranitica

Solanum

" *Many gardeners grow solanums, perhaps without realising it, for* Solanum tuberosum *is the potato. Yet again, this is a huge genus, mainly South American, mainly tender and mainly very poisonous. On close examination, the rather individual flower form is easily recognisable and attractive. Mainly because of their tender nature, rather few species can be grown as perennials in temperate gardens and, among them, the climbers such as* S. crispum *are best known. I hope, therefore, to interest more gardeners in milder places in* S. laciniatum, *the Australian kangaroo apple.* "

Solanum laciniatum

FLOWERS Long-lasting purple, violet or white flowers, sometimes fragrant.
PERIOD OF FLOWERING Summer to autumn.
NON-FLOWERING APPEAL Some forms are semi-evergreen, with glossy, dark green leaves; some have attractive stems and fruits.
SITE AND SOIL Needs a warm, sheltered site, in full sun to light shade; tolerates any except the very driest soil. Makes a fine specimen plant for a container to be taken under shelter in the winter.
HARDINESS Fairly hardy, tolerating -5°C to -10°C (23-14°F)
SIZE About 1 x 1m (3 x 3ft) after five years, 2 x 2m (6½ x 6½ft) eventually.

■ **PRUNING** Where undamaged by winter cold or in a container, better left unpruned. Where winter damage is experienced, cut back damaged stems and up to one-third of the oldest stems to soil level in spring to promote new growth.
■ **PROPAGATION** Semi-ripe cuttings in early summer or hardwood cuttings in autumn.
■ **PROBLEMS** None.

Recommended varieties

S. laciniatum is an exceptionally beautiful plant, with purple stems and clusters of violet flowers with yellow centres, followed by small egg-shaped fruits that ripen from green to yellow. All parts of the plant are poisonous.

Sophora

" *Sophoras really are quite stunningly beautiful shrubs (with some tree-sized species too) that really should be tried in every mild garden, whether in open ground or containers. They are members of the* Leguminosae, *the pea family, but unlike so many other genera in that family, which seem to me to be pretty but with no real distinguishing features, I find the combination of flowers and foliage that sophoras offer to be especially appealing.* "

FLOWERS Clusters of small white or yellow pea-like flowers.
PERIOD OF FLOWERING Late spring to early summer.
NON-FLOWERING APPEAL Attractive pinnate foliage, rather like that of some ferns; unusual bearded seed-pods form in autumn, in large numbers after a hot summer.
SITE AND SOIL Needs full sun and shelter and a light, well-drained soil.
HARDINESS Varies; *Sophora tetraptera* from New Zealand is barely hardy, tolerating 0 to -5°C (32-23°F). *S. davidii* from China is hardy, tolerating -15°C (5°F).
SIZE About 1 x 1m (3 x 3ft) after five years, 3 x 3m (10 x 10ft) after 10 years.

■ **PRUNING** None.
■ **PROPAGATION** Semi-ripe cuttings in early summer, or seed.
■ **PROBLEMS** None.

Sophora tetraptera

Recommended varieties

S. *davidii* is deciduous with clusters of blue-white flowers. S. *tetraptera* 'Kowhai' is evergreen with clusters of bright yellow flowers in late spring and young branches covered with a yellow down.

Sorbaria

❝ *The name* Sorbaria *means 'resembling sorbus' and, although I suppose this is true of the foliage, which is reminiscent of the* Sorbus aucuparia *group of species, the flowers are wholly different. They are much more accurately described by the plant's common name of False Spiraea. The cascades of tiny blooms that make up the large inflorescences can be spectacular in late summer and these are plants that really are best grown as specimens rather than lost amongst other plants in a border.* ❞

■ **PRUNING** Cut back the oldest one-third of the stems to soil level each year in spring.
■ **PROPAGATION** Semi-ripe cuttings in early summer, or removal of suckers.
■ **PROBLEMS** May become invasive.

FLOWERS Large clusters of tiny cream- or yellow-white flowers.
PERIOD OF FLOWERING Midsummer to early autumn.
NON-FLOWERING APPEAL Attractive light green pinnate leaves with silvery undersides, turning yellow in autumn.
SITE AND SOIL Best in full sun to light shade and a rich, moist, deep, well-drained soil.
HARDINESS Very hardy, tolerating at least -20°C (-4°F).
SIZE About 2 x 2m (6½ x 6½ft) after five years, 4 x 6m (13 x 20ft) after 10 years.

Recommended varieties

S. *sorbifolia* has cream-white flowers in mid- to late summer. S. *tomentosa* is rather more vigorous with yellow-white flowers; var. *angustifolia* is a form with brown-purple twigs.

Sorbaria kirilowii

SPARTIUM

Spartium junceum Spanish broom

❝ *For those to whom the name broom provides an image of the small-flowered species of* Cytisus *or* Genista, *this is the other broom.* Spartium *is a one-species genus that originated in the Mediterranean but has now become naturalised in warm, dry regions in other parts of the world. While most of the* Cytisus *and* Genista *brooms are early flowering, this one, with its larger, yellow flowers takes over in summer and continues the theme through to the autumn. It is an easy, undemanding shrub.* ❞

FLOWERS Small inflorescences of long-lasting, fragrant yellow pea-like flowers.
PERIOD OF FLOWERING Mid- to late summer.
NON-FLOWERING APPEAL Dark green, reed-like stems with tiny leaves; small silver-green seed-pods in autumn.

SITE AND SOIL Best in full sun or light shade; thrives particularly well in coastal areas. Best in an alkaline soil but tolerates any as long as it is well-drained.
HARDINESS Moderately hardy, tolerating at least -15°C (5°F).
SIZE About 2 x 1m (6½ x 3ft) after five years, 4 x 3m (13 x 10ft) after 10.

■ **PRUNING** On established plants, cut back all of the previous season's growth to within 15cm (6in) of the base in spring. Old and leggy plants may be cut back hard close to soil level in spring; *Spartium* responds to this whereas *Cytisus* and *Genista* don't.

■ **PROPAGATION** Semi-ripe cuttings in early summer, or seed.
■ **PROBLEMS** None.

Recommended varieties
Normal species only is available.

Spartium junceum

Spiraea

❝ *Spiraeas are probably the most widely grown and planted of all summer-flowering shrubs, although the bulk of the plants will be the vivid red flowered 'Anthony Waterer'. I always think it a pity that the very best spiraeas are earlier flowering and, by summer, are past their best. Nonetheless, if you want a workhorse of a shrub, not very subtle but no trouble either, then a summer-blooming spiraea will provide it.* ❞

FLOWERS Clusters of white, pink or red flowers.
PERIOD OF FLOWERING Late spring to late summer.
NON-FLOWERING APPEAL Some varieties have golden leaves; most have yellow autumn foliage.
SITE AND SOIL Best in full sun but tolerates medium shade; any but the driest or most alkaline soil.
HARDINESS Very hardy, tolerating -20°C (-4°F).
SIZE The tall forms will attain about 1 x 1m (3 x 3ft) after five years, 2 x 2m (6½ x 6½ft) after 10 years; the dwarf forms will attain about 40 x 50cm (16 x 20in) after five years, 60 x 70cm (24 x 28in) after 10 years.

■ **PRUNING** Prune immediately after flowering by cutting back the oldest one-third of the shoots to soil level; those few that flower after midsummer should be pruned in early spring by cutting back all shoots to about 20cm (8in) above soil level.

■ **PROPAGATION** Semi-ripe cuttings in summer or hardwood cuttings in winter.

■ **PROBLEMS** Aphids.

Spiraea nipponica 'Snowmound'

Recommended varieties

Spiraea cantoniensis 'Flore Pleno' is a tall, arching shrub with double white flowers along its branches in early summer. *S. japonica* is available as several dwarf varieties, all flowering from midsummer onwards: var. *albiflora*, dense clusters of white flowers; 'Anthony Waterer', bright crimson flowers and foliage that is sometimes curiously variegated with cream and pink; 'Gold Mound', small heads of pink flowers and yellow foliage; 'Nana', tiny heads of pink flowers; 'Shirobana', deep pink-and-white flowers. *S. nipponica* 'Snowmound' is a medium, mound-shaped shrub with white flowers smothering its branches in early summer. *S. x vanhouttei* is a graceful, arching shrub with dense white flowerheads in early summer, and foliage that is plum coloured in autumn.

Staphylea Bladdernut

❝ *This is a truly magnificent shrub; a pity about the name. But I confess that it creeps into this book under somewhat false pretences; it is a shrub, albeit a large one, and it does have summer interest. But the interest is not precisely in respect of its flowers, for it tends to bloom in spring and, by the beginning of summer, the best is over. Later, as autumn beckons, the beautiful, inflated bladder-like fruits appear and then look really spectacular, especially if the plant is grown as an isolated specimen.* ❞

FLOWERS Clusters of fragrant white flowers.

PERIOD OF FLOWERING Late spring and late summer (see my comments above).

NON-FLOWERING APPEAL Grey-green pinnate leaves, glossy underneath; dramatic translucent bladder-shaped seed capsules.

SITE AND SOIL Needs full sun or light shade; best in a fertile, neutral to acid soil, will tolerate some alkalinity.

HARDINESS Fairly hardy, tolerating -10°C (14°F), but may suffer some damage in severe weather.

SIZE About 1.5 x 1m (5 x 3ft) after five years, 5 x 2.5m (16 x 8ft) after 10 years.

■ **PRUNING** None essential except to remove shoots damaged in the winter.

■ **PROPAGATION** By seed or by layering.

■ **PROBLEMS** May be difficult to establish.

Recommended varieties

Staphylea colchica is the species most likely to be seen; others occasionally offered are generally less hardy.

Staphylea colchica

STEPHANANDRA

Stephanandra

" *Many years ago, I was given a small cutting of a plant which I had heard of but never grown. Never has any shrub so quickly endeared itself to me and proved its worth. It was a selected form of* Stephanandra incisa *and, although I had known and grown other types of stephanandra over the years, this one rapidly proved itself as one of the most effective and attractive of ground-covering shrubs. I've since recommended it widely and do so again now.* "

FLOWERS Profuse small clusters of green-white flowers borne on older wood.
PERIOD OF FLOWERING Early to midsummer.
NON-FLOWERING APPEAL Foliage turns orange and yellow in autumn; attractive arching winter stems.
SITE AND SOIL Needs sun or partial shade, and any but the driest soil.
HARDINESS Very hardy, tolerating at least -20°C (-4°F).
SIZE About 50 x 60cm (20 x 24in) after five years, 1 x 1.5m (3 x 5ft) after 10 years.

■ **PRUNING** None needed, especially when used to form ground cover but, on isolated specimens, cut back up to one-third of the oldest flowering shoots after flowering to promote new growth.
■ **PROPAGATION** Semi-ripe cuttings in early summer, hardwood cuttings in winter or by removal of rooted layers.
■ **PROBLEMS** None.

Stephanandra incisa 'Crispa'

> **Recommended varieties**
> *S. incisa* 'Crispa' is smaller and much better than the normal species, making excellent ground cover, with crinkled, deeply cut leaves.

Styrax

" *Why aren't snowball trees more widely grown? They seem to have so many of the virtues that the modern gardener looks for, being medium-sized shrubs that slowly become small trees, easy to care for, and reliable in flowering if rather slow to get into their stride. Perhaps it is simply their slowness that has worked against them for it has mitigated against nurseries and garden centres being willing to stock them; and in turn, gardeners have never been confronted with their appeal. I hope that after reading this, more people will ask for them.* "

FLOWERS Fragrant, bell-shaped white flowers with yellow stamens hanging underneath all branches.
PERIOD OF FLOWERING Early summer.
NON-FLOWERING APPEAL Light green foliage turns yellow in autumn; small dark green fruits follow flowers in autumn.
SITE AND SOIL Does best in light shade but tolerates full sun; is best in a light, acid soil, but tolerates some alkalinity.
HARDINESS Hardy, tolerating around -15°C (5°F).
SIZE About 1.5 x 1m (5 x 3ft) after five years, 6 x 4m (20 x 13ft) after 10 years.

■ **PRUNING** None.
■ **PROPAGATION** Seed or layers.
■ **PROBLEMS** Very slow growing.

Styrax japonica

> **Recommended varieties**
> *Styrax japonicus* is the most widely available. *S. obassia* with terminal inflorescences of fragrant white flowers that appear occasionally.

Syringa Lilac

❝ Are lilacs really shrubs or are they small trees? I'm never sure and I'm also never sure that they earn their place in the garden. They are certainly wonderful to look at and to smell for a brief period in early summer but, thereafter, the blooms die particularly gracelessly and the foliage is at best dismal. Having said all of this, there's no denying that they have a firm place in gardeners' hearts and, for many a book on summer-flowering shrubs could not be without them. ❞

FLOWERS Large, fragrant inflorescences of single or double flowers in white, pink, blue, red or purple.

PERIOD OF FLOWERING Late spring to early summer.

NON-FLOWERING APPEAL None.

SITE AND SOIL Best in full sun but tolerates medium shade; any but the most alkaline soil.

HARDINESS Very hardy, tolerating at least -20°C (-4°F).

SIZE Varieties of *Syringa vulgaris* will attain about 1.5 x 1m (5 x 3ft) after five years, 5 x 5m (16 x 16ft) after 15 years; the others mentioned here will attain only half this size or less.

■ **PRUNING** Suckers should be pulled away in spring and autumn, and, if possible, dead flowerheads removed after flowering. Up to one-third of the oldest shoots may be cut back to soil level in spring each year or the plant may be left completely unpruned.

■ **PROPAGATION** Semi-ripe cuttings in late summer; not by removal of suckers, which will be of the common lilac used as a rootstock.

Recommended varieties

S. x *josiflexa* 'Bellicent' has huge clusters of rose-pink flowers, and markedly dark green leaves. *S. meyeri* 'Palibin' is a slow-growing small shrub with dense clusters of single pink flowers. *S. microphylla* 'Superba' has profuse clusters of pink flowers from late spring to early autumn and small leaves. *S. patula* 'Miss Kim' is small to medium sized with blue-white flowers that open from purple buds from late spring to early summer, and dark green leaves with curled edges. *S. vulgaris* (Common lilac) has produced many fine varieties among the best of which are: 'Andenken an Ludwig Späth' (syn. 'Souvenir de Louis Spaeth') with magnificent long wine-red inflorescences; 'Charles Joly' with double, dark purple-red flowers; 'Katherine Havemeyer' with double, purple-lavender flowers, fading to pale pink; 'Firmament' with pale blue-mauve flowers; 'Madame Antoine Buchner' with double, rosy pink or mauve flowers; 'Madame Lemoine', a long-time favourite, with pure white double flowers that open from cream-yellow buds; 'Mrs Edward Harding' with profuse wine-red double flowers tinged with pink; 'Vestale' with white flowers, probably the best white, certainly the best single white.

■ **PROBLEMS** Normally none, although it may tend to suffer from a die-back and leaf wilt of unknown cause in late summer.

Syringa vulgaris 'Madame Lemoine'

TAMARIX

Tamarix Tamarisk

❝ I had an unusual childhood in the sense that one of the first shrubs I ever saw was a tamarix. Before I could walk, my gaze was fixed on this plant which grew in the garden opposite ours. Nothing particularly unusual in this you might think, except for the fact that we lived in the centre of England, almost as far as it's possible to be from the sea. The feathery, pink flowered Tamarix, then as now, is generally thought of as a genus of coastal plants and indeed it is at the seaside that you will see it most, but it is much more durable than is often thought and it makes a very pretty specimen or screening plant for all except the coldest gardens. ❞

FLOWERS Long, feathery inflorescences of small pink flowers.
PERIOD OF FLOWERING Late spring to early summer or late summer.
NON-FLOWERING APPEAL Pretty small leaves which may be glaucous, light or blue-green, and give some yellow autumn colour although they are rather bare in winter.
SITE AND SOIL Thrives especially well in coastal areas: needs full sun or very light shade, and a fertile, light, well-drained soil.
HARDINESS Hardy, tolerating -15 to -20°C (5 to -4°F).
SIZE About 1.5 x 1.5m (5 x 5ft) after five years, 3.5 x 3.5m (11 x 11ft) after 10 years.

■ **PRUNING** None essential, but in order to prevent plants becoming leggy, early-flowering types should be pruned after flowering by cutting back the oldest one-third of the shoots by at least half; and late-flowering types should have all the old flowering shoots cut back by at least half in spring.
■ **PROPAGATION** Hardwood cuttings in early winter.
■ **PROBLEMS** None.

> **Recommended varieties**
> T. ramosissima 'Rubra', deep pink flowers, opening from purple buds on the current season's growth, in late summer to early autumn, with glaucous foliage on red-brown stems. T. tetrandra, inflorescences of pink flowers on the previous year's growth in late spring to early summer and green foliage on dark stems.

Tamarix tetrandra

Vaccinium

❝ Vaccinium is a big genus of very useful acid-loving shrubs. They are useful in the sense that many of them yield valuable fruit, but few are grown for their ornamental appeal. Even those that are tend to be endorsed for their autumn foliage colour and rare indeed is the occasion when they are recommended as summer flowering shrubs. This is a small gesture towards correcting that state of affairs for, in a small garden with very acid soil, they can add valuably to the overall appeal. I stress small garden, not because of the size of the plants but because their rather small flowers are then more likely to be noticed. They get lost in bigger places. ❞

FLOWERS Small cylindrical or bell-shaped flowers, white, pink, red or yellow.
PERIOD OF FLOWERING Early spring or summer.
NON-FLOWERING APPEAL Foliage may be evergreen or grey-green, may give autumn colour, with attractive, sometimes edible, fruits.
SITE AND SOIL Needs full sun or very light shade, and an acid to very acid, moist soil.
HARDINESS Most forms are hardy or very hardy, tolerating -20°C (4°F).
SIZE Larger forms will attain about 1 x 1m (3 x 3ft) after five years, 4 x 4m (13 x 13ft) after 10 years, but the dwarf forms may attain only 10 x 20cm (4 x 8in).

- **PRUNING** None.
- **PROPAGATION** By semi-ripe cuttings, seed or layers.
- **PROBLEMS** None.

Recommended varieties
V. cylindraceum is semi-evergreen with clusters of yellow-green flowers tinged with red opening from red buds in late summer and autumn and followed by blue-black fruits. *V. glaucoalbum* is evergreen with grey-green leaves that are blue-white underneath, clusters of pale pink flowers in late spring and early summer and black fruits covered in a blue bloom that lasts into winter. *V. moupinense* is a dwarf evergreen with urn-shaped, deep red flowers on red stalks in late spring and early summer, followed by purple-black fruits. *V. nummularia* is a more tender dwarf evergreen needing shade and shelter, with arching stems and leathery, rounded leaves, deep pink flowers in late spring to early summer followed by edible black fruits.

Vaccinium nummularia

Viburnum

❝ *No book on shrubs can ignore* Viburnum, *a genus that probably includes more garden-worthy shrubs than any other. It's true that their most celebrated attraction is the winter flowers of some species and the rich evergreen foliage of others. But it can't be denied that there is a viburnum for every month and some of those that I recommend for summer appeal could equally well be featured in books on winter foliage, too. For overall appeal, the genus takes some beating.* ❞

FLOWERS Clusters of white flowers, sometimes tinged with pink, sometimes very fragrant.
PERIOD OF FLOWERING Early summer to early autumn.
NON-FLOWERING APPEAL Most have attractive foliage, either evergreen and glossy, or deciduous with rich autumn colours; many also have masses of long-lasting fruits.
SITE AND SOIL Most thrive in full sun to medium shade, and in any soil.
HARDINESS Most are very hardy, tolerating at least -20°C (-4°F).
SIZE Varies with variety, but most will attain about 1.5 x 1m (5 x 3ft) after five years and 3-5 x 3-4m (10-16 x 10-13ft) after 10 years, although *V. davidii* will attain only half this size.

- **PRUNING** None essential.
- **PROPAGATION** Semi-ripe cuttings in early summer or hardwood cuttings in winter.
- **PROBLEMS** None.

Recommended varieties
V. davidii has clusters of tubular white flowers in late spring to early summer, evergreen, dark, glossy leather leaves with duller undersides and, on female plants, if a male is nearby, clusters of turquoise-blue fruits. *V. x hillieri* 'Winton' is semi-evergreen with copper-tinged young leaves that turn bronze-red in winter, and cream-white flowers in early summer followed by red fruits that ripen to black. *V. opulus* 'Roseum' (Snowball tree) is a superb plant with globular heads of green-white flowers but no fruit. *V. plicatum* 'Grandiflorum' has large heads of sterile white florets, flushed with pink; the form 'Pink Beauty' has flowerheads that mature from white to pink; 'Summer Snowflake' has lacecap flowerheads in late spring to summer, with deciduous leaves that turn red-purple in autumn.

Viburnum opulus 'Roseum'

WEIGELA

Weigela

❝ *There is, I think, only one shrub still surviving that was growing when I bought my garden in its neglected, run down state, some 15 years ago. And that shrub is a weigela. What this says, apart from the fact that I like it, is that it is a durable survivor. And so it is with weigelas in general. They are seldom spectacular but they seldom let you down and if nothing else, they serve to fill gaps in the border.* ❞

FLOWERS Profuse funnel-shaped flowers in white, yellow, pink or red.
PERIOD OF FLOWERING Late spring to late summer.
NON-FLOWERING APPEAL Some forms have variegated foliage, some give autumn colour, some have attractive seedheads.
SITE AND SOIL Best in full sun but tolerates light to medium shade; any soil.
HARDINESS Very hardy, tolerating at least -20°C (-4°F).
SIZE About 1.2 x 1.2m (4 x 4ft) after five years, 2.1 x 2.1m (7 x 7ft) after 10 years.

■ **PRUNING** None essential, but mature plants will benefit from having the oldest one-third of flowering shoots cut back to soil level after flowering.
■ **PROPAGATION** Semi-ripe cuttings in late summer or hardwood cuttings in winter.
■ **PROBLEMS** None.

Recommended varieties
Weigela 'Bristol Ruby' is one of the most popular forms, with abundant ruby-red flowers. *W. florida* 'Versicolor' has cream-white flowers that mature to red. 'Eva Rathke' is slow growing with long-lasting crimson flowers with yellow anthers. 'Mont Blanc' is vigorous with large, fragrant white flowers. 'Newport Red' is a smaller form with large red flowers.

Weigela 'Eve Rathke'

Xanthoceras sorbifolium

" *Sorbifolium means 'with leaves like a sorbus'. An accurate observation if you think of* Sorbus aucuparia *but not of* Sorbus aria. *In reality, the foliage is rather more delicate and feathery than that of any mountain ash but it is of course its flowers, spanning the boundary between spring and early summer that gain it an entry here. They don't seem to gain it an entry into many gardens and this is mysteriously one of the Chinese shrubs that has never truly become popular. It will, in time, make a biggish tree but, if pruned carefully, it can also be a most attractive medium-sized shrub.* "

FLOWERS Upright clusters of fragrant white flowers with carmine eyes.
PERIOD OF FLOWERING Late spring to early summer.
NON-FLOWERING APPEAL Large pinnate foliage giving some yellow autumn colour.
SITE AND SOIL Needs full sun to light shade; thrives in any soil, even if extremely alkaline.
HARDINESS Fairly hardy, tolerating -10°C (14°F).
SIZE About 1.5 x 1.5m (5 x 5ft) after five years, 4 x 4m (13 x 13ft) after 10 years.

Xanthoceras sorbifolium

■ **PRUNING** None essential but in limited space, can be kept smaller. Remove the oldest one-third of the shoots to soil level after flowering each year.
■ **PROPAGATION** Seed or hardened cuttings in winter.
■ **PROBLEMS** May well be slow to establish.

Recommended varieties
Normal species only is available.

Zenobia pulverulenta

" *Zenobia is a bit of an oddity, and not just because it is one of the few shrubs with a name beginning with 'Z'. It is a one-species North American genus in the Ericaceae family and, when it is seen, it is generally in the company of its larger and more showy relatives like* Rhododendron. *It is pretty hardy, pretty easy to grow and, I think, simply pretty. There is no excuse for any acid-soil garden not having it.* "

FLOWERS Pendulous clusters of white bell-shaped flowers with a sweet scent, reminiscent of aniseed.
PERIOD OF FLOWERING Early to midsummer.
NON-FLOWERING APPEAL Blue-grey foliage covered in bloom when young, turning orange-red in autumn.
SITE AND SOIL Best in light to medium shade, and an organic acid soil.
HARDINESS Fairly hardy, tolerating -10°C (14°F).
SIZE About 60 x 60cm (24 x 24in) after five years, 1.2 x 1.2m (4 x 4ft) after 10 years.

■ **PRUNING** None essential but may usefully be trimmed after flowering to maintain a neat and compact shape.
■ **PROPAGATION** Semi-ripe cuttings in early summer, or layers.
■ **PROBLEMS** None.

Recommended varieties
Normal species only is available.

Zenobia pulverulenta

INDEX

INDEX

PHOTOGRAPHIC ACKNOWLEDGMENTS

All photographs taken by Andrew Lawson, except the following:
Professor Stefan Buczacki back cover, 1 top, 19 right
Eric Crichton 18, 35, 46, 65 bottom right, 71 bottom right
Garden Picture Library/Brigitte Thomas 78
John Glover 53 bottom right
Reed International Books Ltd./Jerry Harpur 56
Photos Horticultural 81, 91 left, 93 bottom right
Harry Smith Collection 84

With thanks to the following who allowed their gardens to be photographed for this book:
Pattie Barron, Bath; Pru Bellak, Ludlow, Shropshire; Beth Chatto Gardens, Essex ; David and Judy Bill, Slad, Glos.; Crathes Castle, Grampian; Veronica Cross, Bromyard, Hereford & Worcester; RHS Gardens, Rosemoor, Devon; Shan Egerton, Hay-on-Wye; Gothic House, Charlbury, Oxfordshire; Nori & Sandra Pope, Hadspen Garden, Somerset; Penelope Hobhouse, Dorset; Mr & Mrs Simon Johnson, Middle Chinnock, Somerset; Kellie Castle, Fife; Christopher Lloyd, Great Dixter, Sussex; Madingley Hall, Cambridge; Gillian Naish, Charlbury; John and Pauline Napper, Shropshire; New College Oxford; Overbecks Gardens, Devon; Powis Castle, Powys; RHS Gardens, Rosemoor, Devon; RHS Gardens, Wisley; the late Sam Hollings, Charlbury, Oxfordshire; Savill Gardens, Windsor, Berks.; Dr James Smart, Marwood Hill, Devon; Lady Stucely, Hartland Abbey, Devon; Susan Thomson, Spelsbury, Oxfordshire; University Botanic Garden, Oxford; Rosemary Verey, Barnsley House, Glos.; Waterperry Gardens, Oxfordshire.